"Highly recommended! This book is loaded with Robert Collier's proven strategies for improving your response rates, writing more effective sales copy, and making more money.

Better yet, it contains dozens of great sales letters personally selected by Collier for their remarkable selling power. And he tells the inspiring story behind nearly every one.

Brad Petersen, Direct Response Copywriter
www.bradpetersen.com

"Being in the Internet Marketing Business if you don't understand copywriting and your core customers desires they simply will not buy!

Spare yourself the pain and hardship of reinventing your business over and over, this course gives you the business tools, human elements and real examples on how-to go about succeeding, step by step!"

Claudia Medina, Co-Founder
www.peermomentum.com

ROBERT COLLIER

HOW TO MAKE MONEY AT HOME
IN SPARE TIME BY MAIL
In Seven Lessons

AND

MILLION DOLLAR SALES LETTERS
For Your Own Use and Profit

Best Success And Marketing Books Edition
Edited by,

Bernie Malonson

North Audley Media
USA

LCCN: 2008926748

ISBN: 978-0-9816432-0-5

TABLE OF CONTENTS

HOW TO MAKE MONEY AT HOME
IN SPARE TIME BY MAIL

MILLION DOLLAR SALES LETTERS

FOREWORD

By DENSION "DENNY" HATCH

When Bernie Malonson sent me an advance copy of Robert Collier's "lost" masterpiece, *"How to Make Money At Home In Spare Time by Mail in Seven Lessons,"* I was instantly hooked.

One reason for dot-com bust at the end of the last century—where an estimated $4 trillion went up in smoke—was inexperience. Quite simply many of the hotshot twenty-something-marketers, writers, Web designers and merchandisers--did not have a solid grounding in the basics of direct marketing. They did not know how to make an offer, how to ask for an order and make it easy to order.

One of the poster children of the Dot-Com Boom was Jay Walker, the peripatetic founder of priceline.com. Walker was the 1999 Direct Marketer of the Year at the Direct Marketing Days New York annual conference. Jay's luncheon speech was a stem-winder. As described by David Shepard in the July issue of Direct, "Priceline.com founder Jay Walker stunned an audience at Direct Marketing Days in New York this spring by describing a new DM business model—one with close to zero printing, production, postage, lettershop and customer service costs. The message from DMDNY's direct marketer of the year was clear: Welcome to DM over the Web."

Jay's message was not happy news for printers, paper salesmen, list owners, proprietors of lettershops and the folks at Pitney-Bowes. At the conclusion of his talk, the entire audience was ready to slash our wrists.

Jay Walker was proven wrong on two counts:

1. That year the stock of priceline.com hit a high of $165 and closed out the year 2000 at $1.31. Jay lost his job and his company.

2. With the passage of the CAN-SPAM law and the inception of Do-Not-Call telemarketing lists, old-

fashioned direct mail is right back on top as the workhorse of direct marketing.

AN EXAMPLE OF THE VALUE OF
ROBERT COLLIER'S LOST MASTERPIECE

Here is one of the most important paragraphs in the entire book.

> "On a small test like 1,000 pieces, it will probably cost you $40 or $50 to mail 1,000. On big mailings of 25,000 or more, however, you can probably get this cost down to between $30 and $35 a thousand. And it is on the basis of a large mailing that you must figure your results."

This is important for two reasons:

1. This book was published in 1947 when it was possible to be in the mail for $50 a thousand (postage, printing, paper, inserting, list rental). Today it is more like $500/M. All of Collier's advice and information is valid today; just remember he was operating on 1947 dollars.

2. The last sentence in the paragraph is one of the most important pieces of advice you will ever get. Tests cost money. With tests, you are investing in proprietary information about your product or service, offer and lists. Once you have favorable test results, you will want to do a mailing—larger than the first test—to confirm those results. If the confirming test also brings in responses at an acceptable cost-per-order, then you roll out and cash in. However, it is imperative that you do two sets of financial projections at the outset: (1) the tests (which will be expensive) and (2) the rollout, where you will save huge money on postage and more money on paper and printing because of the economies of scale. The budget based on

rollout numbers is the one that must be presented to management. Tests generally lose money; rollouts make money.

COLLIER, THE VISIONARY

All I can say is that sure wish I had this direct marketing classic when I was starting out—or midway or late in my career. Robert Collier was a Renaissance direct marketer—one who became expert in all facets of the business—the mechanics of the medium as well as the messages that will bring in prospects and customers.

Although his letters were mass-produced, they sounded personal. They were emotional, something that today's crop of copywriters seem to be afraid of. Collier used anecdotes and examples and sucked the reader in with his very believable promises. He generated excitement. Forty years after the first publication of this book freelancer Malcolm Decker codified the technique pioneered by Collier:

The letter is likely to be the only "person" your market will ever meet—at least on the front end of the sale—do don't make him highbrow if your market is lowbrow and vice versa. Make sure he speaks your prospect's language. If he's a Tiffany salesman, he writes in one style; if he's a grapefruit or pecan farmer or a beef grower, he writes differently ('Cause he talks "diffrunt.") I develop as clear a profile of my prospect as the available research offers and then try to match it up with someone I know and "put him in a chair" across from me. Then I write to him more or less conversationally.

With *"How to Make Money at Home in Spare Time"* you will have a series of epiphanies that will change the way you think and market:

- His letter that talks about cutting out the middleman can work for any product or service. (Page 17)

- "So don't let any sign of impatience creep into your collection letters," Collier counsels. "Depend instead upon good nature and cajolery to persuade him to pay." The collection series that follows is made up of masterpieces. (Page 31)

- The "black raincoat" story that will show you the thought process involved in taking an existing product and repackaging it for a whole new audience (as opposed to going through the trouble and expense of creating a new product for a new audience. (Page 38)

- The absolutely new (to me!) way of phrasing a money-back guarantee. (Page 75, third paragraph)

- The story of how F.W. Fitch built a multimillion-dollar business starting with just $45.00. (Page 167)

- The effectiveness of premiums. (Page 203)

- Fifteen million-dollar sales letters. (Page 215)

- And everything in between!

Hey! Stop reading this Foreword and start reading Robert Collier.

He will revolutionize your approach to direct mail marketing.

Good hunting!

Denny Hatch
February, 2008

INTRODUCTION

By ROBERT COLLIER

There is a man down in Florida living on the shores of a lake amid groves of fragrant orange trees, who has a unique way of making a living.

His tools are a pencil and a pad of paper. With these simple instruments, he writes friendly, human letters that scores of merchants send to their customers each month to hold their trade, to build good will, to increase their sales. Many of them have doubled their volume of business since using his letters.

Those same tools can earn greater profits for any business, and can be used to start a business from nothing and build it to where it will bring you a comfortable income for the rest of your days.

Perhaps you have heard the story of the young telegraph operator in a crossroads country town who wanted to build an independent business of his own by mail?

He had no money, and his salary was so small that he could hardly make ends meet. But he decided that he had to risk some of that scant salary if ever he was to get anywhere. So he bought $5.00 worth of postage stamps and then in spare time penned letters to other telegraphers along the line, telling them about a low-priced watch he could get for them at a special price.

Soon he began to get back orders, and as each one came in, he sent part of the money to a watch factory with instructions to deliver the watch direct to the buyer, and then he put the rest of the money into more postage stamps. Before many months, he was making so much money selling watches that he gave up his job as a telegraph operator, and devoted his time entirely to building a business by mail. That telegraph operator's name was Richard W. Sears, and his business today is known as Sears Roebuck & Company, the largest and most successful mail order house in the United States.

Such things could be done years ago perhaps you are thinking, but there are no such opportunities today. You are wrong. There are thousands of little businesses springing up all over the country today.

U. S. Government economists estimate that the next few years will show a new, all-time high record for business activity. The volume of industrial production should be the biggest this country has ever known. That will mean bigger pay envelopes, more spending, and better opportunities for new businesses than ever before.

You may have heard of the Buffalo man, who failed in business, lost all his money, and while he was looking around for a job, decided that he might eke out a livelihood by selling ties by mail. He set his family to work sending out letters offering ties, while he borrowed money from friends to buy the ties and pay the postage. Before two years had passed, he had made some hundreds of thousands of dollars out of his tie sales!

You may have heard of Davis of Gloucester, the man who sells fish by mail. He used to go down to the fishing boats as they came in pick out the fattest mackerel, and ship them himself to the customers who answered his personal letters. He had only $200 when he started, and he borrowed that., He has since sold as much as $2,000,000 worth of fish BY MAIL in a single year. Today he has over 200,000 customers, who buy all manner of sea food from him by mail.

You have heard of John Blair of Warren. He borrowed $100 for the postage to mail his first 10,000 letters and now has a business worth millions. His sales of shirts and coats and traveling bags and the like amount to more than $5,000,000 a year.

You may have heard of Larkin, who made soap on his own kitchen stove, and sold it so successfully that he gradually built up his business into the million dollar class. Or possibly of Post, who peddled his own Postum in the beginning; of Eastman, who had little but a new process for coating photographic plates; of Vick, a small town druggist who put together into one solution everything he had ever heard of which seemed good for colds, and made a vast fortune out of it; and of a hundred others who have built great businesses out of nothing but an idea.

> Yes, I have heard of all these, you are probably thinking, *but where do I come in?* Let me ask you this: Have you ever wished that YOU could start a little business of your own and develop it to where it would bring YOU a nice income for the rest of your days, and free YOU from all your present-day cares and worries? You have of course, we all have. So here's where you come in.

There are certain basic fundamentals on which selling by mail is founded. Those fundamentals are the same today as they were 50 years ago. Methods may change, products and styles and tastes may vary, but the basic fundamentals remain the same. Learn them, and you have gone a long way towards learning how to build a profitable business of your own by mail. Learn them, and there is nothing to keep you from following in the footsteps of Sears and Ward and Blair and Davis and all the other successful builders of business by mail.

How can you learn them? The surest, quickest way is to LEARN BY DOING. Start a little spare time business of your own by mail, even though you start it on a dime. It is far better to start small. You are bound to make some mistakes in the beginning, and if you start small, they won't cost you much, whereas if you plunge in ignorantly, you may lose everything you have.

Start small, but START! Remember, the road of 1,000 miles begins with one step. As the poet so aptly expressed it;

"Are you in earnest? Seize this very minute;
What you can do or dream you can, begin it!
Boldness has genius, power and magic in it.
Only engage, and then the mind grows heated;
BEGIN.... and then the work will be completed."

LESSON I

THE VALUE OF A DISTINCTIVE OFFER

Suppose you have no money, no friends or relatives who will lend you any, and no means of raising even a few dollars of capital on which to start. Suppose you have nothing but the ambition to have a business of your own. What could you do?

Well, I'll tell you what others HAVE done under like circumstances.

Some years ago, in Buffalo, E. P. Beaumont failed in business and lost everything he had. While waiting to be released from bankruptcy, he kept looking around for a job or for any way of earning a living for his family.

In the course of his wanderings, he came across a manufacturer of knitted ties which, at the moment, happened to be popular. That gave him an idea. Why spend money for store rentals, salesmen and the like? Why spend ANYTHING on selling expense? Here was a product that was stylish and that every man must have. Why not send it to him without waiting for an order? Why not put so low a price upon it, that men would be glad to accept it and send him the money?

He decided to try it. He persuaded the manufacturer to trust him for a small quantity of ties, he got credit from a printer for the necessary envelopes and printing, and he managed to dig up enough cash for postage. Then he and his family set to work picking from directories the names of men who would be likely to wear such ties, and whose occupation or residence indicated that they should be good prospects.

When a hundred envelopes were addressed, Beaumont put into each three ties, with a short letter telling what a bargain they were, and asking the reader to try them on, wear them, and then enclose $1.50 in the return envelope he was sending, and mail it back to him.

More than 70% of those envelopes came back, with $1.50 in each. 20% sent back the ties. The remainder paid no attention, neither returning the ties nor remitting the $1.50. So here is the way the results shaped up:

Cost of 3 ties @ 19 cents each	$0.57
Envelopes and letter	$0.03
Postage	$0.06
Subtotal	$0.66

Total Cost for 100 packages	$66.00
Postage on 20 returned packages @ .07 each	$ 1.40
	$67.40

Less salvage on 20 returned packages @ .57 each	
	$11.40

Net expenses	$ 56.00
Received from 70% Cash Remittances	$105.00
Net Profit on 100 packages mailed	$ 49.00

There was money in that. With those figures to show, Beaumont went to his manufacturer and his printer and got all the ties and all the printing he wanted. His friends put up as much money as he needed for postage. Within a few months, from being bankrupt, he was on Easy Street. Within two years, he is said to have made well over a million dollars.

The letter that follows was not one used by him, but it is the type of letter that sold these ties by mail, and it is one that was later used with great success by competitors of his.

* * *

Mr. Business Man,

It costs half the selling price of most good neckties just for the "middleman" between the manufacturer and you.

That's why those fashionable new Crepe ties, made of pure silk mixed with the best Upland yarn, sell in retail stores at 75 cents to $1.00 apiece.

If only we could cut out all that needless "middleman" expense, we could deliver these ties to you by mail at less than half that price—*only 33 1/3 cents apiece!*

So we are trying this experiment. Here are three Crepe neckties, in the most popular Spring patterns, wrinkle-proof and pin-proof. These are the same kinds that sell in a retail store for 75 cents to $1.00 apiece. By sending them to you direct-by-mail, *we can give them to you for less than half that price!*

Just put your check or a $1.00 bill in the enclosed envelope and drop it in the mail. Or, if the offer should not appeal to you, slip the ties back into this envelope, paste the enclosed prepaid reply postage label over your name and address, and mail them back to us for full credit.

But if ever you have railed at the high cost of living, this is your chance to bring it down. It's up to you! This is only an experiment with us. If you and enough other men are in sympathy with the idea, we will use it to save you money on other things, too.

It is for you to say. May we have your answer now, TODAY?

Yours for SAVINGS,

* * *

Why didn't many other people try his method? They did, and so enthusiastically that they became pests. I know one man who mailed out 500,000 boxes of Christmas Cards in this way during a single holiday season, and cleared a couple of hundred thousand dollars. I know another who mailed 600,000 bottles of perfume, hundreds of thousands of initialed handkerchiefs, compacts, lip-stick and the like. It came to be so bad that you couldn't go for your morning mail without a wheelbarrow to carry the unordered merchandise.

That couldn't go on. Better Business Bureaus started a campaign against it and the Post Office frowned upon it. No definite law has been passed to stop it, so far as I know, but the Post Office does not permit it on any large scale. Charitable enterprises are permitted to use this method and the chances are that no objection would be made to it if done in a small way, particularly among friends and acquaintances. If all mailings were confined within one state, so as to make the business intra-state, there is some question as to whether the Post Office could stop it, even if they wanted to. But anyone who tried to do a national business on it would quickly be stopped.

It lends itself readily, however, to the building of a small local business. Suppose, for instance, you were a woman and knew how to make unusually delicious candies. The surest way to convince anyone of this is to let him try them. So you make up a batch. You get some small self-mailer boxes from the Mason Box Company of Attleboro Falls, Massachusetts. You put in a quarter pound of candy, individually wrapped in wax papers. You enclose an envelope addressed to you, stamped with 3 cents postage. Then you send with it a letter like the following.

* * *

Will You Try This Box of *Home made Chocolates...*
At My Risk?

Dear Reader,

I'll bet you've never tried home-made Chocolates like these.

Made of purest liquid Chocolate, mixed with real dairy butter, eggs and thick yellow cream fresh each morning. Every piece made by hand, with never a bit of machinery touching it from the first ladle of honey or sugar to the final wrapping of each separate piece. A luscious assortment of cream, honey and nut centers, hand dipped in thick, heavy rich chocolate coatings.

If you've never tasted my home-made chocolates, you have a treat in store for you. TRY them!

If you like them if you think, as so many do, that they are the most delicious chocolates you have ever tasted, just put your name on the back of this letter, wrap 25 cents in it and return in the attached envelope. Otherwise, just put down your name and address anyway, say you didn't care for the chocolates, and owe me nothing.

Yours for a treat,

P. S. To get a full 1-lb. box of these delicious, home-made chocolates just enclose $1.00 with your name and address. That's the regular price for a pound package, but if you send it, we shall be glad to have you keep this sample package as our treat—FREE.

* * *

All this done, you address your boxes to carefully selected names in business offices. Secretarial workers, typists, clerks, business men, all like a bit of candy after lunch, all have money to spend and are good credit risks. I know one woman who built up a candy business of over $100 a week in a comparatively small town in just this way. Later she used it to sell cookies, cakes, etc., and when she had a large enough group of customers she opened a Tea Room which, at the time she sold it to a big competitor, employed eighteen people.

Suppose you were good at embroidery. You could use the same plan to sell initialed handkerchiefs, as with the following letter:

* * *

Dear Mr. C,

When you leave the office tonight, you won't feel any the worse for it, if during the day you have granted two simple requests to a friendly little handkerchief girl.

The requests are:

1. Will you look at the four hem-stitched handkerchiefs I'm sending you in this letter, embroidered in two colors of silk with *BOTH your initials,* and see how they compare with those you've bought in stores for 50 cents or more apiece?

2. Please, Mr. C, if you like them enough, send me not the store price of 50 cents or more each, but just half that, only $1.00 *for all four!*

But, of course, if you don't want to keep the handkerchiefs even at this price, just put them in the envelope and mail them back to me. I am enclosing a prepaid reply postage label, so that I'll not be imposing on you.

Thank you ever so much for your courtesy!

Your friend,

P. S. I am also enclosing a prepaid reply envelope to put your $1.00 in to pay for these hand-embroidered handkerchiefs. Just write your name and address below, wrap your check or $1.00 bill in this letter and return it in the return envelope enclosed.

I'll be eternally grateful to you.

Your name

Address

City   State

* * *

And to those who bought, you could then send more expensive items such as Bridge Covers, Luncheon Sets, Table Cloths, etc.

Or suppose you had a line of Cosmetics. Wouldn't this be a good plan to introduce the first item, using a letter like the one that follows?

* * *

Dear Madam,

You don't know me from Eve, but I have been told

that you love nice things, that you have bought them in the past and that apparently you like them.

If this is so, you must have taste and judgment, and you must know what fine toiletries, vanity cases and the like should sell for. You are able to measure not only their value, but their intrinsic worth in dollars and cents.

What, then, do you think a dainty, attractive compact like the one enclosed, *with your initial on the cover,* should sell for?

How much, in other words, would you personally be willing to pay for this exquisite, little compact, with its delicate fragrance, its subtle air of refinement?

Bear in mind that a compact like this, is not only a personal adornment, but the size and the new shape make it especially convenient to carry in your purse. And your initial on the cover gives it a touch of personal distinction that one seldom finds in any but the most exclusive shops.

I suggest that you compare this Compact with any you see in your favorite stores, estimate what the finished, initialed Compact would sell for, and then look at the enclosed payment form and see how close your guess is to the actual cost!

I shall be very much interested to know what your first guess was, and will appreciate it if you will fill it in on the back of the payment form giving me this information.

Thanking you in advance for this courtesy,

Gratefully yours,

* * *

That would be your opening wedge. To all who bought compacts, you could send lip-sticks, powder, cold creams, and other items of interest.

Or, suppose you started with Perfume. You might send a small 1-oz. vial, using the letter that follows to sell it

* * *

Dear Madam,

Though I have never met you, I am writing to you as one woman to another.

You can help me make a very important decision, and I don't think you will mind doing it when I explain. I know I would gladly do as much for you, if you asked me.

With this letter I am sending you a full-ounce, gift-package bottle of lovely Perfume (the personal choice of many discriminating women!) and a dainty Handkerchief of fine quality.

Will you *TRY* this Perfume for me on the Handkerchief I'm sending you?

You'll be under no expense or obligation. I just want you to tell me whether you like it or not.

Because we are planning to SELL it to women all over the country, if this little test shows that a majority of these selected to try it, like yourself, *really like it.*

This Perfume is selling for $4.00 and $5.00 an ounce in the exclusive shops of Fifth Avenue, Palm Beach, Newport and other places, where society and fashion leaders gather. These women have already given it the stamp of their approval.

But, are *they* typical in this respect, of the thousands and thousands of American women, who are NOT the wives or daughters of millionaires? Will American women *as a whole* like this Perfume well enough to buy it, if we can save them money, at say, $2.50 an ounce?

Please break the seal on the bottle of Perfume I'm sending you and put just a drop or two on the Handkerchief.

Hold the handkerchief at arm's length and move it gently so the full fragrance of the Perfume is wafted toward you.

Now — DO YOU LIKE IT?

If you *don't,* just put the Perfume and Handkerchief back in the box and use the enclosed prepaid reply postage label to return them to me.

And, I'll be deeply grateful to you for helping me with your opinion!

But, if you DO like the Perfume so well that you would like to KEEP it for your own, just send me in the enclosed envelope only $1.00—to help pay the expense of this test—and keep the Handkerchief, too, with my compliments!

But, PLEASE don't return the Perfume without trying it! Your opinion will mean a lot to me either way, and it doesn't cost you a penny to TRY it. Don't disappoint me.

And, of course, I'm in a big hurry to know how you vote, so we can make our plans about selling the Perfume on a larger scale.

Won't you let me have *your* answer *quickly?* Within the next two or three days?

Gratefully yours,

* * *

That would open the way to higher priced items or to other toiletries. You see, your first sale is like the first olive out of a bottle, or a maid's first kiss . . ., hard to get. But those that follow are comparatively easy. Once you have sold a customer a single item, and satisfied him , he is yours. You can sell him anything else in reason that he needs. So even if you were to make no money at all on your first sale, it would still be highly profitable, because you could immediately follow it up with other sales.

Just to show you exactly the method to use when you want to ship merchandise without an order, I shall take Christmas Cards as an example and show you the complete mailing and follow up.

1. Go to your local Postmaster and ask him for a permit to use pre-cancelled stamps. You need these for parcel post packages. Get from him at the same time a circular showing the postage rates on 3rd and 4th class matter. If your envelope

or package weighs less than 8 ounces it can go out at 3rd class rates 1½ cents for each 2 ounces. If over 8 ounces, it must take parcel post rates of 8 cents for the first pound in the first zone, increasing with each pound and each zone.

2. Remember to use envelopes or mailing containers that can be opened for Post Office inspection, and if you ship parcel post, print on the container or on the shipping label, "Contents—Merchandise. Postmaster: This parcel may be opened for postal inspection if necessary. Return Postage Guaranteed."

    Then if the one to whom it is addressed should refuse it, or should have moved, you will get back the package promptly, but will have to pay the same return postage that you paid to send it.

3. Where you have enough profit margin, it will pay you to use a prepaid reply envelope. This is the kind on which your customer need put no stamp. You pay the Postman 4 cents when he delivers it to you. You need a special permit to use this Prepaid Reply Envelope. In most places, such a permit costs you nothing, but some Postmasters require a deposit of $10.00 to insure them against loss if you should fail to pay the Postman when he delivers your mail to you. Just ask the Postmaster for the form to use in applying for permit to print prepaid reply envelopes.

These are the preliminaries. Your address can be a post office box, or your home, or your place of business. The address itself is of little consequence. People doing business with you by mail seldom have any way of knowing whether your address is the finest business building in town or the poorest tenement section, so don't squander money on high rentals just to get a ritzy address. It isn't worth it . . . when you sell by mail. Do everything as well as you can, but inexpensively.

Rich paper, fine printing, a lot of color, are not worth their extra cost. Don't let your material look cheap, but don't let it run into expense, either. Plain printing, medium price paper, one or two colors, will ring you as good results as the most expensive make-up. After all, it is the message that counts, the bargain you have to offer, the price you can give, etc. Here is the way it was done with Christmas cards.

To begin with, remember that people can buy nice Christmas Cards at the 5 cent and 10 cent stores, or at the nearest stationers, for prices ranging from two for a nickel on up. Yet you've got to get $1.00 for your package of cards, because $1.00 is about the lowest unit of sale at which you can hope to show a profit. And of that $1.00, your cards and wrapping and postage should amount to not more than 33 1/3 cents leaving the balance for selling cost and profit.

To get any large number of orders on so competitive an item as Christmas cards, you have to make your offer distinctive. You must have something that the 5 cents & 10 cents store or the corner stationer does not yet give with his. Yet your gift cannot cost you much, or you'll go beyond your limit of 33 1/3 cents. What can you give that sounds like a lot of value, yet costs you little?

Books lend themselves to such a gift, and you can often pick up odds and ends of discontinued editions for a song. Almost any publisher has some such books that he will be glad to be rid of. Pictures lend themselves even more readily to such offers and any lithographer can dig up scores of subjects that he will let you have for 2 cents or 3 cents each. Here is a letter based on such an offer.

In the upper left hand corner of your letterhead, paste a miniature reproduction in color of the picture you are going to give as a premium. (Such a premium, by the way, is not essential to trying out the sale of Christmas cards in this manner, but it does help the returns materially.) Then reproduce your letter.

* * *

"To be Remembered by a Friend is
One of the Pleasantest of Human Experiences"

Dear Friend,

I take pleasure in submitting for your approval this ADVANCE MAILING of fourteen new and most attractive Greeting Cards—the fourteen we have picked as the most distinctive and beautiful of all the thousands of designs submitted to us.

In years past we have sent out Christmas Cards, beautiful cards, distinctive and cheery, but never before have we been able to put into them so much of friendly feeling, so much of warmth and individuality, as in those we have gathered together for next Christmas. These Christmas Cards have an easy and heart-warming way of expressing their friendly greetings. Your friends will remember and appreciate them as never before. They bring home as no ordinary card can the fact that this is not a mere perfunctory greeting, but that you are really thinking of them, wishing them well, sending them thoughts of friendship and love.

No expense has been spared to make this the finest assortment of Christmas Cards at any price. The 1947 vogue calls for simpler and more modernistic design, beauty of paper stocks, richness of engraving, and more cheerful, friendly sentiments.

Notice how these Deluxe Greetings have all these smart up-to-date features. Every card is the fashionable French Folder style. A rich variety of newest handsome decorated and metallic paper stocks help to bring out the beauty of the designs. Six cards have genuine steel engraving and there is nothing finer in the graphic arts. The artistically styled, hand-lettered greeting texts and sentiments are warm and friendly, radiating good cheer and the true Christmas spirit.

I hope and believe you will share my enthusiasm for these beautiful Greetings. You will not find their like plastered over every gift counter and stationer's *window* in the country. If they were obtainable in stores, you'd pay $1.50 to $2.50 each for these cards. They cannot be bought in any store, because they are exclusive designs, yet by remitting at once, you get them, NOT at $1.50 to $2.50 each, BUT ALL FOURTEEN FOR ONLY $1.00 apiece.

Of course, there is but little margin in that for us. If it were not for the kindly co-operation of our customers, we could never make ends meet at that figure. But by sending your $1.00 right away you cut our bookkeeping costs to practically nothing and enable us to come out ahead.

Just your personal check or $1.00 in the enclosed envelope will pay for all 14 of these distinctive and beautiful cards. Won't you fill in the handy payment blank enclosed, pin your $1.00 to it and mail it back NOW?

Thank you. I am counting on your friendly cooperation.

Gratefully,

P.S. Will you accept, as our gift, a large reproduction

in full color of the famous painting shown in miniature at the top of this letter? Just as an appreciation of your courtesy, I am going to send you a large size reproduction of this famous painting, suitable for framing, as soon as I receive your $1.00 payment for the enclosed cards. I think you will regard the picture alone as being well worth $1.00.

———————

Directions: These cards are sent to you on approval. To keep them send us $1.00, using the payment blank and our addressed envelope which are enclosed.

If you wish to return them you will find postage-paid reply label enclosed. Just replace the box in the carton as you received it, pasting the addressed label on it and mail. If you keep the cards beyond the usual week's examination period, I will assume you are keeping them and will send payment promptly.

On receipt of your payment, the full color reproduction of the famous painting shown in miniature at the top of this letter will be sent to you, postpaid, as our gift.

* * *

Then enclose with your letter a Payment blank addressed to you and reading about as follows:

* * *

I enclose $1.00 in full payment for the 14 lovely Christmas Cards you sent me. On receipt of it, you are to send me a large reproduction in full colors, suitable for framing, of the famous picture shown in miniature on your letterhead.

Name

Address

City   State

P. S. I am enclosing $_____ extra, for which please send me additional boxes and pictures.

* * *

Two weeks after mailing your box of Christmas cards, if you have not heard from the recipient with remittance or return of the cards, you can start your series of collection letters, mailing them a couple of weeks apart.

Remember, though, the customer did not order these cards from you. He is under no legal obligation to return or pay for them. So don't let any sign of impatience creep into your collection letters. Depend instead upon good nature and cajolery to persuade him to pay. Here is the type of letters that have brought home the bacon for others, and that should do the trick for you.

* * *

Dear Customer:

The gladdest words of tongue or pen in these days are:

"Enclosed find check!"

It's a mighty small bill you owe us for those cheery

Greeting Cards (I wish it were more) but just the same, it will come in handy.

For when you send us a dollar, we pay it over to our printer, he passes it on to the paper manufacturer, who uses it to pay his workmen, and they in turn buy food and clothing with it, so that every dollar keeps working day in and day out, adding to the volume of business and' building up prosperity.

So the dollar you send us will be a productive dollar, a hardworking dollar, a dollar that will roll back again to you by and by, and probably bring other dollars with it.

Will you bring that happy day nearer by starting him on his way NOW?

Gratefully,

* * *

Dear Customer:

When an account runs much past its due date, we find that most of our customers appreciate a brief note from us, reminding them of the fact, so they may remedy the delinquency.

Accounts like ours are so much out of the regular routine that we can readily understand how they may be overlooked.

Now that we have called your attention to it, I am sure you will be glad to wrap a dollar bill in this letter and return it at once in the enclosed envelope as full payment for those fourteen distinctive Greeting Cards that we sent you some weeks ago.

I'll be eternally grateful to you if you will.

Yours anyhow,

* * *

Dear Customer:

The only thing in the wide world we can find the matter with business is this:

THERE IS NOT ENOUGH
MONEY IN CIRCULATION!

This condition can be easily remedied, if everyone will do his share—and we'll gladly do ours if you will do yours.

If you will send the $1.00 to cover the box of Christmas cards we mailed you, we will immediately keep it circulating. Then we will both sleep better for having done our share to put business back on a normal basis.

Yours—for mutual co-operation,

* * *

Dear Customer:

We've been told that a certain fastidious young lady living near us kneads bread with her gloves on.

That may sound unusual, but we are in far worse

case. We need bread with our shoes on. We need bread with our hat on. And unless a few good customers like you come to our help with the $1.00 for that box of Christmas Cards we sent you, we'll need bread without anything on it at all.

R. S. V. P. Just write your name and address across the back of this letter, wrap a dollar in it and mail.

Yours hopefully,

* * *

Dear Customer:

Have you heard this one of Bud Fisher's?

"For the love of Mike!" exclaimed Jeff, looking at a letter.

"Bad news in the letter, Jeff?" asks Mutt.

"I'll say so. Terrible news. A fellow writes me that he wants my autograph."

"I'd call a request for my autograph a compliment."

"You wouldn't if you got this one," replied Jeff. "He wants my autograph on a check for the fifty bucks I owe him!"

May we not, like Jeff's creditor, request your autograph on a check for $1.00 (or just a plain dollar bill will do) covering the box of cheery Christmas Cards we sent you a month or more ago?

Appreciatively,

* * *

Five such follow-up letters should bring in $1.00 from most of those you have sent your cards or other merchandise products to. Certainly it will bring either the dollar or the return of the merchandise from about 90% of them. And if it brings the $1.00 from something like 70%, you should make a profit out of it, and at the same time be building a list of customers who will buy other products from you in a highly profitable volume.

Where to get your Christmas Cards? Look up in the Classified Directory of your Telephone Book the names of Christmas Card manufacturers. Write to them. Or look on the back of some of your old Christmas Cards and see if the manufacturer's name and address is not given there.

You can try this out in a small way first, writing the letters that are to go with the cards in long-hand or on your typewriter. If in longhand, make the letters short, so as to be easily read. And remember, though long-hand letters take time to write, they get the highest response of any kind of letter you can send.

So don't be ashamed of having to start small, and write your letters yourself. That is the way Richard Sears started, and look at the size of Sears Roebuck & Company today. A. T. Stewart started what is now the John Wanamaker New York store on a capital of $1.50. You can start your business on a postage stamp. The great thing is to *start*.

AND HERE, WE BELIEVE,
IS THE ONE SAFE, EASY WAY TO START.

Let us suppose you don't want to take the chance of mailing out goods without an order. (It is a chance, of course, and we know that it cannot be done on a large scale, because the Post Office will object to it unless it is done locally or at least within the state where you live.) Or suppose you have no particular product in mind and don't know how or where to find one that will sell readily by mail. What then?

THEN LESSON II OF THIS COURSE
WILL SOLVE YOUR PROBLEM.

For Lesson II is written around definite offers, the best we have seen as far as the margin of profit to you is concerned and the best-pulling offers we know in addition.

These offers do not require you to take chances. They need an initial investment on your part of not more than $2.00 or $3.00. If you are satisfied with the results from that small investment, you can go ahead on a larger scale. If not, you'll be out little if any.

The first of these offers is a book on Guerilla Self Defense. It sells for $1.00, and of that $1.00, you get 75 cents. All you have to do is to get the order with the $1.00 payment, and send that order, accompanied by 25 cents, to us. We will immediately send the book to your customer, postpaid.

But that isn't all! To those who buy this book, you can then offer either fast-selling books on health lines, two of which are given in Lesson II. Again you keep a generous part of the money you receive for them, sending the balance to the publishers, and they deliver the books, postpaid.

Lesson II shows you exactly how to get the names of people concerned about their health, it gives you small "Classified" Ads to use in getting them, tells you where to insert them and how, and then provides the tested, proven letters for selling the books to these people and for selling them later volumes.

That is one of the offers in Lesson II. It sells easily, because it relates to the Health, and of all products, those having to do with Health sell most readily by mail. Not only that, but of all good mail order lists, those of people who have bought Health products are most plentiful.

But perhaps the best part of it is that once they have bought one Health book from you, they make the very best prospects in the world for other books on Health. You can follow them up time after time, selling them other books or other health products, and build a business that should bring you a profitable income for the rest of your days.

Lesson II has what we regard as some of the best offers in this whole course. But every one of the seven lessons has definite, proven offers that can be used practically word for word to start a business of your own by mail, and to start it NOW.

Remember, there has never been a time when the average American had as much money in his pocket as he has today. There has never been a time when he was ready to spend it as freely for the things he wants. If you want to build a business of your own by mail, a business that should bring you a goodly income for the rest of your days, now is the time to start.

Just as an evidence of the possibilities and increasing importance of selling by mail, the Department of Commerce has prepared a manual, *"Establishing and Operating a Mail-Order Business."* This may be obtained from the Superintendent of Documents, Washington 25, D. C., or from Department of Commerce Field Offices, for 25 cents. Among the topics discussed are; The nature and scope of a small specialty mail-order business, selecting a line, merchandising plans, and legal aspects.

Also available are the following leaflets: *"Planning to Start a Small Mail-Order Business"* and *"Mail-Order Business—Basic Information Sources."* These will be sent free on request to the Division of Printing Services, Department of Commerce, Washington 25, District of Columbia.

LESSON II

IDENTIFY LOGICAL PROSPECTS

I don't pretend to be a prophet, but I'll tell you who is going to make a lot of money in the years of good business that economists predict lie just ahead.

It's the chap who masters, the art of getting business by mail. Depend upon it, he will be the key man in the new order of things. Already business is reserving its richest rewards for the practical mail merchandiser. And why shouldn't this be so? A man, who can sit at his desk and develop more actual orders than a hundred salesmen out pounding the pavements, surely is a valuable asset to any organization.

There is a firm in the northwestern corner of Pennsylvania with an interesting bit of inside history.

Thirty-five years ago this firm consisted of one man. Today there are several hundred employees, but it is still a one-man business. It has never employed a salesman on the road, and it has never employed any collectors. The head of the firm has never been out to call on any of his customers.

Yet this firm is known everywhere.

Sitting alone in his office, the head of this firm was one of the first to foresee, 35 years ago, the real possibilities of the letter. He saw that if he could write to a man a thousand miles away the right kind of a letter, he could do business with him as well as with the man in the next block.

He began with undertakers. Working his way home from college a short time before, he had earned money selling raincoats to small town merchants. In one store, he had an inquiry for a black raincoat, and on asking why anyone should want a black coat, was told it was for an undertaker. That started him to thinking.

Here was a little town with only one or two undertakers in it. They must have black raincoats, but stores could not afford to carry them because nobody else wanted such an uninteresting article. There must be thousands of undertakers like that scattered all over the United States. If one central store could cater to them all, it would be able to carry the necessary stock to offer a full assortment of sizes, at prices no higher than the average store charged for a coat of the usual yellow variety. He decided to try it.

There was no difficulty in inducing his factory to make up 400 black raincoats. Borrowing $100.00 for postage, he and his brothers sent out 10,000 letters to undertakers, offering black raincoats at the price in effect for common yellow ones.

Needless to say, the 400 coats went and 400 more on top of them. In fact, a third 400 was ordered before he was able to fill all the orders received from that first direct mail effort of his.

Then one day a Catholic Priest wrote him. "Dear Sir: At a funeral last Tuesday, it rained cats and dogs and all of us were soaked except our esteemed undertaker, Mr. Josiah Simmons. He had on one of your black raincoats and was dry as toast. Have you any such coats suitable for Clergymen?"

That opened a new field. For the next few years, black raincoats were in demand not only by undertakers, but priests and ministers. The young man's sales grew accordingly. Presently, some of his satisfied customers began to ask for other articles of wearing apparel, like shirts and socks and the like, so he stocked these, too. And, when the stocks became varied enough, he branched out to serve other occupations; lawyers, doctors, engineers, accountants.

He began *talking* by mail to men everywhere who he thought might buy his goods. Talking to them in sane, human, you and me English. Through those letters he sold goods. Nor did he stop there. In the same human way he collected the money from them, he addressed any complaints that arose. He did everything that any business man could do with customers. In a few years he was talking not to a thousand men, but to millions. Today though few men have ever seen him, this man's personality has swept like a tidal wave across this country and left its impression in office, store and factory through letters, letters alone.

You too, can do this with letters. But to do it requires three essentials

1. **The Product or Idea you are to sell.**
2. **A list of logical prospects.**
3. **The right copy in your letter and circular.**

Each of these three essentials is important, and no one has yet been able to figure out which is most important but of the three, perhaps the most difficult is a list of the people most likely to buy your product.

Many people have an idea that if they get a good letter about a product that is in general demand, they can send it to a list of names taken from a telephone directory or to automobile owners or people with good incomes, and get a satisfactory response. Nothing is farther from the truth. In thirty years' experience, selling all manner of products by mail, I have not found half a dozen that could be sold profitably to telephone or automobile lists.

As a general proposition, the best prospect for your product is someone who has bought by mail a product of a similar nature from someone else. For instance, the best prospect for a book relating to health or foods is someone who has bought by mail order books relating to health, or a physical culture course, or some health foods or vitamins or remedies.

It is easy enough to get such lists. There are list brokers in most big cities who make a specialty of it. Here are a few of the best known list brokers.

Mostly Selective List Service, 38 Newbury Street, Boston, Massachusetts.

D-R List Bureau, 80 Broad Street, Boston, Massachusetts.

Willa Maddern, 215 Fourth Avenue, New York, New York.

Arthur M. Karl, 25 West 45th Street, New York, New York.

Chart Letter Service, 208 N. Wells Street, Chicago, Illinois.

The usual charge for the use of fresh mail order names, i.e., recent buyers of books or other products by mail, is 1 ¼ cents to 1 ½ cents each. That cost adds materially to the price you pay for circularizing, but it usually gives you two or three times the results you would get from an ordinary list.

There is a way, however, in which you can start from scratch and build your own lists. That way is through the Classified Advertising columns of your newspapers and of a few special magazines.

Let us suppose that you want to start a mail order business; that you have no special product in mind; and that you have very little money. What product lends itself best to such a situation?

In my experience, the most likely product for you is books! Books have a wide appeal. Books have a big margin of profit. Books require small inventories and can be shipped more cheaply than any other product I know of.

But what kind of books? Not fiction, certainly, for there you are competing with every corner bookstore. But self-improvement books of some kind.

Books and courses showing how to develop your body have always been good sellers, as witness the huge business done by the great muscle builders like Jowett, Atlas, Liederman, etc. Books on sex have a wide appeal. Books on how to make more money, how to get ahead, how to improve your position, all sell well.

Right now, because of the publicity given to such methods by the commando and ranger training, one of the best sellers we know of is books on Jiu Jitsu, Judo, or Guerilla Self Defense.

Guerilla Self Defense of New York, ran a series of advertisements newspapers and magazines which, on the average, brought back in cash or C.O.D. orders *double their cost!* On the following pages are copies of two of their advertisements.

These ads were run in the *N. Y. Mirror* Sunday edition, in a number of groups of Detective magazines, in *Popular Science* and *Mechanix Illustrated* and in a number of the comics. In the comics, they were run in full pages, in the magazines as single columns, in the newspapers as a two-column spread.

As they stand, they are complete in themselves, doing their own selling and bringing back the cash or C.O.D. order. And as stated, they are paying for themselves twice over. The resultant orders are good not only for the immediate profit they pay you, but as the most valuable thing in any mail order business, a list of customers who have bought from you, who have been satisfied with what they bought, and who therefore will listen with attentive interest to any other offer you may make to them.

To put an ad the size of those above in most newspapers or magazines, however, would cost you in the neighborhood of $100 or more. And many of our students will not want to risk that much as a starter.

To them, our suggestion is, start your advertising in the Classified Columns of newspapers and magazines, using the "Personal" column, or the "'Business Opportunities" or "Instruction," and putting it in preferably on a Sunday. For such an ad, use only a few lines. Don't try to "sell" your reader, just endeavor to win his interest sufficiently to get him to drop you a card asking for further particulars. You ought to be able to get such inquiries at an average cost between 5 cents and 10 cents apiece. Here is the type of advertisement you could use.

* * *

I BROKE HIS HAND LIKE A MATCH!

It was easy. He howled with pain. It was amazing how quickly I turned the tables on the thug with this simple, bone-smashing hold! Learn the amazing secrets of Guerilla Self-Defense, based on natural, instinctive impulse action. Send a card for FREE particulars. (Your name.)

or

I BROKE HIS FINGERS—LIKE TWIGS

Out of the dark, I felt the brutal strangler's grip. In a flash, he was paralyzed with broken fingers, even though he was twice my size. Learn this new method of offensive defense, based on natural, instinctive impulse action. Send a card for FREE particulars. (Your name.)

* * *

You could take every one of the 70 bone-breaking secrets given in the book on Guerilla Self Defense, and make a separate ad of it. You could use one of the thumb-nail sketches to illustrate each ad, and thus get greater attention value. But however you do it, you should be able to bring back a steady stream of inquiries, costing you not more than 10 cents each, and possibly as little as 2 cents or 3 cents.

To these you must then send a selling letter, and it helps if you accompany the letter with a reprint of one of the advertisements shown the earlier pages of this lesson. Any printer can make a photo offset of these ads inexpensively, and run off a few hundred or thousand for you. Or you can get printed copies of the ad quite cheaply from George Talbot of Norwood, Massachusetts. Mr. Talbot makes a specialty of printing letters given in this course, and his prices are lower than any we have found elsewhere for small quantities.

Here is suggested copy for your sales letter:

* * *

If This Should Happen To You,
Would You Know This Quick Defense?

Dear Customer:

The Associated Press reported from Los Angeles a short time ago that an attractive 20-year-old telephone operator was walking down the street late one evening, when a thug suddenly grabbed her from behind.

What would you do if that happened to you? Most women, certainly, would, just yell, or faint, or struggle fruitlessly, while the thug took their valuables and worked his will with them. And many men would be just about as helpless.

But not Mary Bischel! She quickly leaned forward, grabbed the thug's ankle, then reared back and planked him flat on the pavement. Then she stomped on his face and fled.

Now that the Commando training of soldiers has made so many people familiar with the tricks of Jiu Jitsu and Judo and Guerilla Self Defense, you read of such incidents frequently. There was the case of Private James E. Stokesbury of Seymour, Connecticut, as an instance.

According to the police, a holdup man named
Montgomery followed Isidore Gitler and his payroll
of $2,200 into an elevator, and when he got out,
stuck a revolver in his ribs, grabbed the payroll and
dashed down the stairs.

Gun in hand, Montgomery ran into the crowd at
Broadway and 37th St., but he made the mistake of
roughly jostling Private Stokesbury, who was
passing with his wife. Stokesbury gave Montgomery
the "hip mare," slamming him down on the
pavement with a bang, then took the gun away
from him and turned him over to a passing
policeman. "All I needed to throw him," said
Private Stokesbury, "was a hip mare, and boy, it
never fails."

HERE, WE BELIEVE, IS
THE GREATEST SELF-DEFENSE OFFER
EVER MADE!

You have heard of George F. Jowett, who for many
years was the world's strongest man. Even today
many of the records he made have never been
broken. Yet Jowett started out as a cripple and a
weakling! At eleven, he was so badly beaten up by a
bullying older boy, that he was in bed for a week.
But during that week, he resolved to learn how to
defend himself, to learn the tricks that would enable
a weak little fellow like him to hold his own against
any bully that comes his way.

He studied Jiu Jitsu, he learned wrestling and
boxing, he sent for every system of self defense
ever heard of. And he learned that the easiest
methods, the surest and most deadly methods, are

not Jiu Jitsu or Judo or any of the highly advertised systems, but those based on natural, instinctive impulse-action.

Within a short time, he was able to reduce that bully who had licked him so badly, to a whimpering, blubbering baby, whining for mercy. Within ten years, by practicing the methods and exercises he had learned, he became the world's strongest man.

Since that time, George Jowett has been all over the world, teaching, studying, and demonstrating. He has learned the methods of aggression and defense of every nation under the sun. He has taught hundreds of thousands how to rebuild their bodies, how to defend themselves. And from all of his knowledge and experience, he has now picked the 70 methods that, in his opinion, will enable you to hold your own against any thug, any Jiu Jitsu fiend or knife thrower.

Mind you, these are not the complicated, hard to learn methods of the professional wrestler or Jiu Jitsu expert, but simple, proved methods based on natural, instinctive impulse action.

You don't need to depend upon catching your foe off guard. Jowett shows you how to disable your opponent with methods that KNOCK HIM OUT COLD! He teaches you to be ready to deliver a knockout every time without fail. There's no use throwing a man, you know, if he is going to get up and come right back at you. Jowett shows you how to *fix* him so he will stay out! And now he has put those 70 bone-smashing methods into a little book that you can read in an hour, that you can put into practice ten minutes later.

The price? You'll smile when you hear it. Only $1.00, and even that $1.00 has a string to it. You get it right back if you return the *"70 Bone-breaking Secrets of Guerilla Self Defense"* within 5 days. No explanations needed and no questions asked. Return the book and you get your $1.00 back at once.

FREE—"12 Knockout Punches Used by Experts!"

If your order for *"70 Bone-breaking Secrets of Guerilla Self Defense"* is received within 10 days, we will include with them —FREE— a copy of *"Knock 'em Cold!"* revealing the secret of twelve knockout punches of famous champions.

"Knock 'em Cold!" is condensed from a bigger book that formerly sold for $5.00. It has all the meat of the big book, without the expense.

Don't miss this amazing combined offer of TWO valuable books on scientific self-defense, on our 5-day trial! If you are not delighted with them, you have only to return the *"70 Bone-breaking Secrets of Guerilla Self Defense"* to get your money back in full. Just use the enclosed Coupon. But remember, your Coupon must come within 10 days to get a FREE copy of *"Knock 'em Cold!"*

Sincerely yours,

———————

5-DAY FREE TRIAL COUPON

Your name and address

You may send to me the *"70 Bone-breaking Secrets of Guerilla Self Defense,"* by George F. Jowett, for many years the world's strongest man. With it, you are to include a FREE copy of *"Knock 'em Cold,"* containing 12 secret knockout punches of famous champions.

When the Postman delivers the two books, I will pay him $1.00, plus the postage charges. (We pay all delivery charges if you send your $1.00 with this coupon.)

If not satisfied for any reason, I can return the *"70 Bone-breaking Secrets of Guerilla Self Defense"* within 5 days after I receive it, and you are immediately to refund my $1.00 in full. Name, address, etc.

* * *

You can get that letter printed on a letterhead bearing your name and address, from George B. Talbot of Norwood, Massachusetts for a very few dollars. Or, if you want to get the best results, you can type the letter yourself, filling in the reader's name and address, and making a carbon copy of the letter.

Fully half of your inquiries should respond to the original letter. To those who do not, send the carbon copy of the letter a couple of weeks later, with a few lines written on the top with pen and ink, to the effect, "This is your last chance! We have only a few copies of *"Knock 'em Cold"* left. To get one FREE, your order will have to be mailed right away."

But when you get the order, what are you to do with it? Just make out a shipping label to the customer (you can buy stock labels at any stationers), and send it, with 25 cents to Income Builders, 152 West 42nd St., New York 18, and they will immediately ship the two books, postpaid, to your customer.

Or, if your order calls for C.O.D. shipment, send 25 cents to Income Builders, with instructions to send the books to you. Then take them to your post office, and the postmaster will show you how to ship them C.O.D., so that the remittance will come back direct to you.

In other words, Guerilla Self Defense has been selling these books retail for $1.00, but you as a wholesaler and distributor, can get them for only 25 cents from Income Builders, leaving you a margin of 75 cents for your profit. You ought to make good money on that margin.

But that is just the start. Few people figure on making a profit on their first sale to a customer. Most are content to pay something, just to get a man's name on their books. The big mail order houses, for instance, spend $2.00 just to get their catalogues into your hands.

But here is an offer on which you should make money on your first sale. After that, succeeding sales should be easy, for that first sale is like the first olive out of the bottle, the rest follow easier.

But before going into the matter of succeeding sales to these customers, let us first exhaust the different methods of how to make your first sale.

We have covered the "complete-in-itself" advertisement, where all you have to do is to place your one-column ad in some newspaper or magazine, and wait for the orders with money attached.

We have covered the inquiry method, where you use small copy and ask only for an inquiry from those interested. Then to this inquiry you send a sales letter and copy of the complete advertisement, thus getting orders from perhaps fifty or sixty percent of those who inquire.

There is still another method. That method is to buy or rent lists of people who have bought or inquired about other courses (people who have responded to advertisements of Atlas or Liederman or Jowett, for instance) and send to them the same letter you would send to those who responded to your own ads. You would not get anything like as good a response, of course, but if the lists are fresh and good, you should be able to get a profitable response, and if you do, it opens the way to quick sales in goodly quantities. Here is the way to go about it.

First, you pick the list you are going to test. For a small mailing, would be our suggestion that you try 500 names each from the two best lists you can find.

Second, if you have a letterhead, type carefully the letter given in the preceding pages starting, "If This Should Happen To You." if you have no letterhead, put your name and address in capitals at the top of a plain sheet of paper, and let it be your letterhead. If you do this, it would be our suggestion that you get an 8 ½" x 11" sheet of paper and fold it over once, thus giving you a 4-page folded letterhead, each page 5 ½" x 8 ½" in size. Put your name and address at the top of the first page, and start your letter on it, carrying it over to the text three pages. Use single space typing, with double space between paragraphs, and wide margins at the sides of the pages.

When you have neatly typed the four pages of the letter, sign with your name in black ink, and then take it to some printer who can do photo-offset work. For a small test, you will find it cheaper to have your letter photo-offset than to have it set up in type and printed specially for you, though George B. Talbot of Norwood,

Massachusetts, can probably do this cheaper because he is printing the same letter for a number of our subscribers. Mimeographing is also an inexpensive method of doing a small test, and if neatly and clearly done, is just about as effective as printing.

The order form can be typed on a separate half sheet, and photo offset in the same way.

All you now need is a mailing or outside envelope and a return envelope. Turn to Lesson I and see the instructions given for obtaining a postal permit for the use of pre-cancelled stamps and mailing third class, and also for obtaining permit to use a pre-paid reply envelope.

To mail third class under 1 cent postage, remember that the upper right hand corner of your envelope must bear in small type the words, "Sec. 562, P. L. & R." This can be printed in 6-pt. type, but it must be printed on the envelope, just above the space where the stamp is to be affixed. The rules for the use of third class matter will be given you by the Postmaster when he issues your permit.

In the upper left-hand corner of your envelope, your name and address should be printed. This is not essential, but it does look more business-like.

For a small test, it is not strictly necessary that you use prepaid reply envelopes. You can enclose a plain envelope, with your name and address printed or mimeographed on it. Small quantities of envelopes in any size can be bought at any stationers, but for large quantities, you will get better prices by looking up an envelope manufacturer in the classified telephone directory. The size outside envelope that we find most effective is what is called the baronial size about 4 ½" x 5 ½" or 6". The return envelope can be a smaller size baronial, or an ordinary No. 6 envelope folded over.

That gives you all the material for your test mailing. Fold your letter face out, so that the first thing the reader will see when he opens the envelope will be your letterhead, place the copy of the ad on Guerilla Self Defense in the fold of the letter, the order form inside that and the return envelope in it. Then enclose in the outside envelope. If this outer envelope is what is called a "Penny-saver," i.e. with a side flap that can be opened for postal inspection, seal the envelope. If not, just tuck in the flap. You can then put a 1 cent pre-cancelled stamp on it, sort the mailing into groups by cities and states as prescribed in the directions furnished you by the Post Office, and take it to the Post Office for mailing.

On a small test like 1,000 pieces, it will probably cost you $40.00 or $50.00 to mail 1,000. On big mailings of 25,000 or more, however, you can probably get this cost down to between $30.00 and $35.00 a thousand. And it is on the basis of a large mailing that you must figure your results.

For instance if you can get 50 or 60 orders from each thousand mailing, you may not make any money on your first thousand test, but you will make good money on a large mailing. For if you figure the cost of a large mailing at $35.00 a thousand, 50 orders would give you a gross return of $37.50 after paying Income Builders 25 cents each for delivering the books, leaving you $2.50 net profit. And 60 orders would give you $45.00, or $10.00 net profit, on each thousand circulars mailed. That is a return of nearly 30% on your investment. And on numbers of good lists, you should be able to get 60 or even more orders to the thousand.

Not only that, but you should be able to sell at least a fourth of these customers, (and quite possibly half of them), other books on Health and kindred subjects. Follow-up letters with which to do this are given later.

That is the quick way to get started. It involves the immediate spending of at least $40.00 or $50.00, and it is something of a gamble, for no one can tell you whether the lists you have picked

for your test will be productive or not unless he has tried them.
So the safer way, and the one that involves the least risk, is to build
your own list as you go along. This, as before stated, can be done
through the Classified Advertising columns of your newspapers or
of certain magazines. In our experience, the "Personal" column and
the "Business Opportunities" column are the most productive,
though the "Instruction" column sometimes pays out too. And the
only day on which we have been able to get really satisfactory
results is Sunday. If you happen to strike a rainy Sunday, your
results will sometimes be doubled.

The next thing to think of is how to sell these customers of yours
further books, for the real profit in any mail order business comes
from the re-sales..., not from the first sale. Anyone who has bought
such a book as that offered by Guerilla Self Defense is interested in
health and strength, so suppose we offer him next, *"Renew Thy Youth
Like the Eagle"* and *"Secrets of Youth"*. These books sell for $1.00, they
cost you only 30 cents, and you can get them through Income
Builders, 152 West 42nd St., New York 18, N. Y.

Some 50,000 copies of these two little books have been sold. They
are still being sold with great success, but excepting for a few of our
mail order customers, none of it has been done through advertising.
All the sales have been made to regular mail order lists. You can
introduce these books to a brand new market by offering them to
your buyers of *Guerilla Self Defense,* or by advertising them direct in
the classified columns of newspapers and magazines.

Some newspapers pull far better results than others. The most
productive papers we have been able to find are, in the order of
their result-getting abilities *New York Mirror, New York News,
Philadelphia Inquirer, N. Y. Times, Chicago Herald Examiner, Denver Post,
N.Y. Journal-American, Detroit Free Press, Los Angeles Times, Los Angeles
Examiner, Indianapolis Star, Pittsburgh Sunday Telegraph, Memphis
Commercial Appeal, Jacksonville Times Examiner, Fort Worth tar Telegram,
St. Louis Post Dispatch.*

And here are the magazines that pulled best for us: *Pathfinder, Popular Mechanics, Grit, Cappers Weekly, Popular Science Monthly.* On books like *Guerilla Self Defense* that appeal to younger readers, the comics pull best of all.

If you will write to the Chicago Union Advertising Agency, they will send you an Ad-Guide, listing all newspapers and magazines, and giving the rate per line for each.

To the names received from your classified ads, and to lists of people who have bought other books on health, or health products, you could then send this letter:

* * *

Here, I Believe, Is One Reason That Animals Live
More Than Twice As Long, Comparatively, as Man!

Dear Customer:

You know, of course, that animals live to about seven times their maturity. And you know that man matures at eighteen to twenty years of age, so if he lived the span of practically all other animal life, he could reasonably expect to reach an age of 126 to 140 years. Furthermore, he should lose none of his vital forces, he should retain most of his youthfulness and vigor right up to within a few years of his end.

Why doesn't man live that long?

Why does he die, on the average, at three times maturity when animals live to seven times theirs? In our opinion, the one biggest reason is his UPRIGHT POSITION!

Do you know that if you hold a rabbit upright for two hours, it will die? Why? Because of the sagging of its vital organs. Man has been bred to an upright position through hundreds of generations, so it does not kill him quickly, but the pull of gravity on his vital organs tends to make them sag, makes him pot-bellied, gives him jowls like a turkey gobbler, and puts a pressure upon all his organs that crowds them together and makes him an easy victim of all manner of diseases.

The ancient Scriptural writers seem to have understood this, else why should they have adjured us to "renew our youth like the eagle"? The eagle oftentimes lives to an age of 250 years. Why? What does he do that you do not? *He flies with his head lower than this heart!*

The Marathon runners of ancient Greece, whose endurance amazed the world, rested themselves and renewed their energies by lying at the foot of a tree with their feet propped high up against the tree. A dog or a horse or almost any animal will rest with its head lower than its heart. Parrots live to unbelievable ages, and you know how often you have seen a parrot hanging by its feet from its perch, its head down.

You see, old age is in effect a drying up process. And naturally, the parts that dry up first are those that the heart finds it hardest to reach—the nerve centers and glands in the head and the back of the neck which control every vital organ. Let the blood run DOWN to those centers for a time each day, and you give them a chance to "renew your youth like the eagle."

Dr. Donald Laird in his experiments at Colgate University has found that man's brain functions 7% faster and 14% more accurately when the head is lower than the body, than when it is in an upright position. And teachers of physical culture find that they get far better results from exercises taken in a prone position than when standing.

In the past several years, a beauty salon in New York has become famous for restoring youthful figures and even youthful cheeks and chins to fat, middle-aged ladies by a system based primarily on exercises taken with the head lower than the rest of the body!

With my compliments I am going to send you a little book called *"Renew Thy Youth Like The Eagle"* that gives the methods and exercises which, in our experience, can best be used to renew and revivify the glands and nerve centers of the head and neck. There will be no charge for this. It is FREE.

I am going to send this amazing little book to you WITHOUT COST OF ANY KIND . . . just to get you to send for and examine for 31 days Robert Collier's *"SECRETS OF YOUTH."*

This little book contains what seems to me the "meat" of scores of books and courses that promise to tell you how to retain or regain youthfulness It tells you the foods that are said to have rejuvenating effects, the different methods and exercises which some authorities claim will keep you from growing old.

It tells you about the "Bacillus of Long Life,"

discovered by Professor Metchnikoff of the Pasteur Institute in Paris; about the "Royal Jelly" which makes "Queen" Bees out of ordinary worker bees; about Voronoff and his "remedy for old age"; about Vitamin E and its rejuvenating effect on the glands; about science's latest discovery, the Auxinon, and how it tends to grow new and youthful cells.

To buy all the books and courses from which these methods were gleaned would cost you $100.00 or more. Yet you can have what seems to me the "meat" of all of them, the boiled down essentials, for only $1.00. Not only that, but you can examine it, TRY it for 31 days and if for any reason you are not more than satisfied, you can return it at the end of that time, and get your $1.00 back in full.

So you run no risk. And whether you keep the *"Secrets of Youth"* or not, you may have *"Renew Thy Youth Like The Eagle"* FREE . . . *to keep with our compliments!*

Would you risk $1.00 for 31 days to get *"Secrets of Youth"* for which we paid much more than $100.00? Would you spend a few minutes time to get FREE the methods that were practiced with such success by the great men of the Bible for thousands of years?

If you would, then fill out the enclosed Gift Coupon and mail it NOW. This is the last lot of the *"Secrets of Youth"* now in print. You may never be able to buy it again at this low price.

Sincerely,

No. 289

Please return This Coupon At Once!

This coupon, if filled out and mailed at once, entitles the sender to a FREE copy of *"Renew Thy Youth Like the Eagle."*

Your name

Street

City   State

Surely, I shall be glad to examine and TRY OUT for 31 days *"The Secrets of Youth"* provided you will include with it a FREE copy Of *"Renew Thy Youth Like the Eagle."*

You may send them to me by mail.

When the Postman delivers them, I will pay him $1.00 (plus the small postage charges). On this distinct understanding: If I return *"The Secrets of Youth"* within 31 days, you will immediately refund my $1.00 in full, yet I may keep *"Renew Thy Youth Like the Eagle"* , FREE!

Name

Address

City   State

*We pay postage if your $1.00 is sent with this order.

You get your money back just the same if you return *"The Secrets of Youth."*

* * *

When you receive this Coupon from your customer, with $1.00 attached, you can send your label (or just the name and address) to Income Builders, 152 West 42nd St., New York 18, accompanied by remittance of 30 cents and they will deliver *"The Secrets of Youth"* and *"Renew Thy Youth Like the Eagle"* to your customer. If the Coupon comes without cash payment, you can send 30 cents to Income Builders for the books, and they will send them to you. You can then ship them to your customer C.O.D. Your Postmaster will tell you how.

Now you have the start of a customer list, and it is the customer list that is the gold mine in the mail order business. You should be able to sell a goodly percentage of them almost any other book you nay have to offer.

Health lists are among the best lists for any type of mail order merchandise, because they are usually made up of men and women of middle age, who have begun to worry a bit about their physical well-being, and who have a little extra money to spend on themselves. So your health-minded customers are excellent prospects for other products laying to do with health.

So suppose we offer them next a product that all of us need.

In *Collier's* of December 19th, 1942, there was an article entitled, *"The Town Without a Toothache."* It described the town of Hereford, east of Deaf Smith County, Texas, and told how certain elements in the soil kept the teeth of Deaf Smith County dwellers in perfect condition, even rebuilt decayed teeth for newcomers who moved there.

The article was reprinted in *The Readers Digest* the following February, in condensed form.

Few of us who live in other parts of the country have perfect teeth. Few there are who do not have to be continually going to their dentist to have cavities filled. Most of us would give a lot to be sure we could hold on to all the teeth we have left, and if the eating of a few special foods would do it, we'd gladly pay a good price for those foods.

So for those who would like to start a mail order business, I can think of no product more likely to sell than a breakfast food made from wheat grown in Deaf Smith County, Texas. A letter to the Chamber of Commerce of Hereford would bring the names of millers who make such breakfast foods, and you could buy them in quantities at a price that would enable you to sell them at a goodly profit for $1.00 pound, attractively packaged.

I would get the permission of *The Readers Digest* to reprint their two-page article, and I would use it for my circular. Then with it I would mail the following letter:

* * *

Would You Like To Prolong
The Life Of *Your Teeth*
10 Years, 20 Years or More?

Dear Reader:

What would you give to be able to do away with all tooth decay . . . to keep your teeth in perfect condition for the rest of your days? Would you risk

$1.00 on it?

It has been done—IS being done—as you will see from the enclosed article reprinted from *The Readers Digest*. The people of Deaf Smith County in Texas have no such thing as tooth decay . . . and all because of certain elements in the soil of that county.

How would you like to share their immunity from tooth decay? You can do it, food scientists believe, if you will eat foods grown down there.

You see, your teeth are made up of certain elements which, like all the other cells in your body, are continually wearing out. You've got to replace those lost elements, or see your teeth decay. The trouble is that some of these elements are no longer present in the soil of most sections of the country, so we don't get them in our food. Result? Decay! But if we can find soil that does contain all these essential elements, and raise our food in that soil, then we can have sound teeth once more. The soil of Deaf Smith County, Texas, contains every element essential to the growth of sound teeth. And of all the foods grown there, none is richer in these elements than wheat.

From that wheat, we have made a breakfast food rich in every element essential to the health of your bones and teeth. We call it _____.

A generous helping of _____, each morning should provide enough of those elements necessary to the building of sound teeth to keep your teeth in perfect condition. It should provide enough to build strong, perfect teeth for your children, to give them sound, straight bones throughout their bodies. Not only that, but it is an energy food as well, one that will start you on your day's work full of vim and enthusiasm.

Will you try it? A pound package costs only $1.00, postpaid, and if ever there was a package of health and of everything that makes for a sound and perfect body, this is it.

Not only that, but if you are not more than satisfied with it you have only to return what is left at the end of 30 days and we will cheerfully refund your $1.00.

So you run no risk. And if the experience of those who live in Deaf Smith County is to be believed, here at last is the way to be rid of dental decay for good, to have sound teeth for the rest of your days.

Sincerely,

* * *

For your order form, you could use something like this:

* * *

HOW TO LAUGH AT DENTAL DECAY

John Jones
Jonesville, New York

You may send me, postpaid, subject to 30 days' trial, a one-pound package of _____.

I enclose $1.00 in full payment, on this distinct understanding:

If I am not more than satisfied, I can return what is left of this package at the end of 30 days, and you are to refund my $1.00 in full.
Name

Address

Zone No.

City   State

* * *

Few products sell by mail like those having to do with the health. Nearly half of our population today is over forty years of age, and that half is continually on the lookout for means to retain or regain youthful vigor, virility and pep. Thousands of fortunes were made out of patent medicines in the old days. Many are being made today out of vitamin tablets.

You can buy vitamin tablets in bulk from any wholesale drug house. You can have them packaged under your own name. And with some such letter as the following, you can readily sell them.

* * *

Here Is an Energizer That Will Help To Give You
The Secret of Straight Thinking For Success!

Good Morning Sir,

Remember how you used to plow through great masses of work day after day and month after month, cheerfully, with never a sign of tiring or nervous strain? Remember how you used to enjoy those evenings, starting out as fresh from your office or shop as if you hadn't just put a heavy day's work behind you?

No doubt you've often wondered why you can't work and enjoy yourself like that now, but solaced yourself with the moth-eaten fallacy that, "As a man grows older, he can't expect to put the same force and enthusiasm into work or play that he did in his earlier years."

Poor old exploded idea! As if youth were just a matter of time! Genuine youth is a healthy physical state. Genuine youth is a matter of red blood corpuscles and active glands. You can be as brisk, as alert and quick-thinking today as you were ten or twenty years ago. You can bring back the fire and force of youth to your work, if only you will re-activate your glands, re-energize your blood stream.

You may have read of the experiments conducted on animals. For 30 days they were starved by feeding only on refined foods. Then, when they were at the point of death, when their limbs were paralyzed, they were given foods rich in Vitamin B complex. The results were that in a few days they were strong and healthy, full of vigor and pep.

A similar test was made with six healthy people in a famous hospital in Rochester, Minnesota. For 88 days these six people were given foods lacking in Vitamin B-1. And do you know what happened to these six healthy people? They became nervous and irritable. They developed backaches and sore

muscles and couldn't sleep. They complained of
spells of dizziness. They became sad, discouraged
and depressed. Then they were again given Vitamin
B-1, and quickly their troubles were over. They
became their normal, vigorous, healthy selves in a
matter of days.

Why did the U. S. Government supplement the
soldiers' and sailors' diet with vitamins? Why but
for the reason that so many of our foods are
refined and no longer contain the elements essential
to health and strength.

"Entirely without vitamins," says the celebrated
food scientist, John X. Loughran, "human life
would cease. Partially without them, which is true
of the majority of civilized people, life processes
burn with a fitful flame, sickness more or less
serious is the general rule and real health is known
and recognized by but few people." Of all the
essential elements that enter into the building of the
body, perhaps the most important are the B
complex vitamins. Without them, life would be
impossible for any great length of time. They ignite
the chemical elements in the food you eat, and
furnish vital nutrition to every cell. Without them,
you would soon die.

And in tablets, you get a rich supply of Vitamin B
complex. One tablet after each meal supplies twice
the amount of B complex vitamins that are
considered essential each day. One tablet after each
meal for a month should bring you a feeling of
youthfulness and vigor such as you have not known
for years.

Will you TRY them? You can do it entirely at our risk. The enclosed order form will bring you 100 tablets—a full month's supply—subject to 30 days' trial. If for any reason you are not satisfied with the results, you have only to tell us so to get your money back in full.

The price? You'll smile when you hear it. $1.00 for 100 tablets, guaranteed to be rich in the very vitamins that our foods need most—the B complex vitamins. And your $1.00 will have a string to it. It's not ours until you say so. You get it back at the end of 30 days if you are not more than satisfied with the results,

On that understanding, will you mail the enclosed form? On that guarantee, will you DEPOSIT $1.00 with us for one month?

Sincerely,

* * *

Your order form should read:

* * *

On your specific guarantee that I get my money back at the end of 30 days if I am not satisfied, you may send me a package of 100 Vitamin B complex tablets.

I enclose $1.00 in full payment. Please send the tablets post-paid.

* * *

There is one thing, however, that you will have to watch carefully if you sell health books or health products. That is the claims you make for them. You may tell a man that the ear muffs you offer him are better than any to be found in Eskimo-land. You may tell another that your heater will make his house warm as toast, even though it may only heat one small room. You can say pretty much what you like about your products, within reason, and get away with it as far as any government agencies are concerned, but the moment you make claims about health, you will have a dozen government bureaus on your neck.

The American Medical Association seems to have its representatives or ardent advocates firmly entrenched in a number of government bureaus, and they are naturally opposed to anything that savors of self-medication, no matter how good or how harmless it may be. This is especially true of the Solicitor's Office of the Post Office Department. They are out to stop the sale by mail of anything that savors of self-medication, and through the use of the "Fraud Order," they can do it, regardless of the merits of your product.

You see, if you make any claim whatever of what your book or your product will do, they can allege that this claim is exaggerated, and that therefore you are getting money from your customers under false pretenses . . . in other words, defrauding them. And they will thereupon summon you to a hearing to show cause why a Fraud Order should not be issued against you, stopping all your mail.

As the hearing is before one of the Solicitor's assistants, and another one of his assistants is the prosecutor, while Postal Inspectors are the witnesses, you can guess what your chances are of an acquittal. It doesn't matter what backing you have for your claims. Unless they are endorsed by the American Medical Association, they are worthless.

Here, for instance, is a letter offering a product called B-Kelp. If you can find any exaggerated or misleading claims in it, you are a better man than I am. But the Solicitor's Office of the Post Office alleged that it made fraudulent claims, and threatened the proprietors with a Fraud Order unless they discontinued the business.

This is one of the letters referred to by *THE BOOK OF GOLD*. A couple of young veterans used it to start a mail order business, and in the first six months of 1946 they cleared better than $7,000.00.

* * *

WHY GROW OLD?

"The key to mankind's long-sought Fountain of Youth," wrote the *Los Angeles Examiner* some time ago, "may at last be found." For, said the article, Scientists at Cornell University have discovered that certain foods appear to retard the biochemical changes that attend old age and senility.

"Of all such foods," says John X. Loughran, famous food scientist, "those containing IODINE are most important." It has been said— "The age of a man depends upon the quality of his thyroid gland, and in my experience it is true, for the thyroid secretion is the most powerful force known in body metabolism. And the thyroid is entirely *dependent upon IODINE for its healthy functioning.*

"No effort towards regaining the characteristics of youthfulness pays as abundant dividends as adding a small amount of FOOD IODINE to your daily meals."

Man's greatest evil is senility, not death. When his

glands are no longer able to secrete their "Life Ferments," when his blood is too thin and weak to keep his brain cells alert and active, then indeed has old age come upon him. Then is he but the living shell of a man.

But that time can be postponed. And perhaps the most important factor in putting off senility and decay lies in the amount of IODINE in the blood. For it is not only the thyroid that needs Iodine. Blood, glands, liver, all need their quota. IODINE has well been called

"THE ANTI-OLD AGE ELEMENT!"

The great trouble is that so much of the soil in which our foods are grown has been practically denuded of Iodine. Erosion, floods, continual plowing, have washed away most of the Iodine as well as many other elements essential to our well-being. As Dr. Charles Northen put it, "We have been systematically robbing soils of the very substances necessary to growth, and resistance to disease."

In an article in *Readers Digest,* Rex Beach wrote, "Do you know that most of us suffer from dangerous diet deficiencies which cannot be remedied until the depleted soils from which our foods come are brought into proper mineral balance? No man today can eat enough fruits and vegetables to supply his system with the mineral salts he requires for perfect health, because his stomach isn't big enough to hold them."

There is only one place where there has been no

loss of IODINE. There is only one place where the vegetation contains ample amounts of every element necessary to the well-being of your body. That place is the FLOOR OF THE OCEAN!

Meats and fresh water fish contain only 5 parts of Iodine to the billion, potatoes 18 parts, eggs 22 and codfish 240, but Sea Vegetation contains 900,000 *parts of IODINE to the billion!*

Under the direction of John X. Loughran, Pacific Kelp from the floor of the ocean has been dehydrated and combined with natural yeast to make a tablet superlatively rich in IODINE and Vitamins. It is called B-Kelp. Three B-Kelp tablets a day provide an adult's full daily requirement of Vitamin B1 and B2. Three of them give you more than six times as much IODINE as is generally regarded as the daily need.

Says Loughran: "No one needs added minerals and vitamins more than the man or woman who has passed age 37. Lagging energy metabolism, weakened vital reserves, have to be combated more strongly. Fortunately, such people usually respond quickly and dramatically to high vitamin and mineral feeding, resulting in better appearance, more work efficiency.

"Enthusiastic reports of improved energy metabolism and renewed energy have come to me from students who have used B-Kelp the last few months. B-Kelp and B Vitamins are entirely NATURAL, extracted from special strain Yeast.

"B-Kelp Iodine is also NATURAL, harvested from

the best sea plants, not to be confused with medicinal Iodine, which is inorganic. We all need FOOD IODINE daily for our glands, the skin, keeping youthful, resistance to infection, for mental development. Combining the two NATURAL B Vitamins with IODINE creates 'synergistic action' which nutrition science avers increases the potency of both."

TRY B-KELP FOR A MONTH…, AT OUR RISK!

The enclosed 30-day Trial Coupon will bring you 100 B-Kelp tablets (a full month's supply). Their price is $2.98 (3 cents each) but you don't need to worry about that, for your money will have a string to it. It's not ours until you say so. You get it right back at the end of 30 days if you write us that you have taken the 100 tablets and are not satisfied with the results.

Over in the Philippines, years ago, the natives suffered terribly from beriberi (thiamine deficiency). No cure had ever been found for it, though every manner of drug had been tried. A young scientist named Williams made an extract from the hulls of ordinary rice (the part most people had been throwing away) and administered it to the sufferers. At once they revived, and *in a short time were well!*

Why? Because those hulls contained the essential VITAMINS and MINERAL SALTS without which the body cannot function.

Your thyroid gland cannot function without IODINE, and without the thyroid secretions you would soon grow old and die. There was no drug in the extract that Scientist Williams administered to the beriberi sufferers. There is no drug in B-Kelp, no medicine of any kind.

B-Kelp does not produce quick results like a drug. It will not work miracles overnight. Dr. Mitchell Stevens reported in a Medical Journal the results on three other doctors, all men of 58 or over, who tried Iodine in different forms. The first said it had a wonderful effect upon him. The second wrote that he had never been in better health. The third reported his health much improved, and that he felt younger (and his friends told him he looked younger) than for five years.

We do not guarantee that it will have the same effect upon you, of course. Other factors may be involved in your case besides a lack of IODINE. But we do promise you that if you are not more than satisfied with the results, we will refund your $2.98 without question.

On that understanding, will you mail the enclosed 30-day Trial Coupon? *TODAY?*

Sincerely,

* * *

Of course, these two veterans could have appealed the findings of the Solicitor's office by taking it to a U. S. Court, and they would probably have won an injunction restraining the Post Office from interfering with their mail. Other companies selling health products by mail have done this and won their cases, and the veterans' lawyer told them he felt sure they could, too.

However, it would have involved considerable expense, and as they planned to go to college in the Fall, they decided to give up the business, so they sold all their stock on hand to another veteran, after explaining the circumstances to him.

He consulted another lawyer, and was advised not to "sell" the Kelp, but to find some book relating to Food Iodine that he could sell, and then *give away* a month's supply of B-Kelp with each book. The lawyer explained that since the Post office was trying to stop the sale of anything that might be regarded as a self-medication, it would object to his description of B-Kelp, no matter what he might say, and if he was *selling* the B-Kelp, they might make their objections stick. However, there is a well-established legal principle that there can be no fraud without some consideration, and if he received nothing for B-Kelp, he could not be accused of defrauding anyone.

This veteran found a little book called *"IODINE—Nature's Own deterrent to Old Age"* and decided to sell it for $2.98 (the regular price of the B-Kelp) and to GIVE a month's supply of the B-Kelp with it FREE.

So he took the supply of circular letters that had been left over from the previous company's mailings, and across the top of each printed in red script, "A Full Month's Supply FREE! See Special Order Form." He enclosed one of these with each of his circulars, in order to identify the B-Kelp that he was offering FREE and to give the reader some description of it.

Then for his own circular, he printed the following in the form, of a 4-page circular, with the order form on the fourth page:

* * *

FREE —A Full Month's Supply of B-Kelp
If You Are Prompt!

Of all the glands in your body, the only one that requires a special food is the Master Gland (the one that guides and to an extent regulates all the other glands—The THYROID) and that special food is IODINE.

Without this special food, your Thyroid will not function. And without a properly functioning Thyroid, you will quickly develop old age weaknesses and other ailments.

Over in England, where the food problem is so acute, Scientists have been experimenting for many years with food iodine, and some of their discoveries are startling in the extreme.

They believe that "Old Age" can be held off for many years. They have found that the "useful" life of a cow, for instance, may be extended from the average of 5 years to 7 or 8 years, and they believe that the active virile life of man may be extended by perhaps 20 to 25 years. In a little book called , *"IODINE— Nature's Own Deterrent to Old Age"*.

We have brought together the findings of leading scientists of Britain and the world, giving results that have been obtained through the use of food iodine. Not only do they regard iodine as the element that combats "Old Age" and its attendant ills, but they add that mental growth, normal weight and resistance to disease are but a few of the benefits that may come from its use.

TRY IT FOR 30 DAYS AT OUR RISK!

The price of *"IODINE—Nature's Own Deterrent to*

Old Age" is $2.98. It is a small book, and may not on the outside look that value, but when you have read it you will agree that the facts it gives you would be cheap at many times the price.

But that isn't all. With this little book you get— FREE— a month's supply of B-Kelp, 100 tablets that sell regularly for $2.98. Try them for 30 days. If you are not more than satisfied with the results, return the book and your $2.98 will be refunded in full at once.

FREE—While this limited supply lasts!

The Blank Company sold many thousands of B-Kelp tablets at $2.98 for each package of 100 tablets. But they have now given up the business, and we bought their entire stock of B-Kelp tablets at a bargain price. While that stock lasts, you can get a full month's supply FREE merely by mailing the order form on the next page. Their stock was clean and fresh, and has been going rapidly, so if you want a FREE supply, better use the order form SOON!

30-Day Money-Back Trial Coupon

This offer is made possible only because we bought up the entire stock of B-Kelp tablets of the Blank Company at a bargain. It does not apply to any future stocks we may get at regular prices. It is good only if accepted at once.

Such & Such Co.

New York, N. Y.

YES—You may send me, subject to 30 days' trial, a copy Of *"IODINE—Nature's Own Deterrent to Old Age,"* and with it FREE a package of 100 B-Kelp Tablets, sufficient for a full month.

When the Postman delivers them, I will pay him $2.98, plus the postage charges.

On This Distinct Understanding:

At the end of the 30 days' trial, if I am not satisfied with the results, I can return the booklet and you are to refund my $2.98 in full at once.

Name

Address

City   State   Zone No

*We pay postage if you send your $2.98 with this order; you get your money back just the same if you return the book.

* * *

That circular pulled for this young veteran as well or better the letter alone had pulled for his predecessors. In the summer months of 1946, he cleared $5,000. Then came Nemesis in the shape of the Solicitor's office, wanting to know why a Fraud Order should not be issued against him. His lawyer urged him to fight, and assured him that the Post office had not one chance in a hundred of making a Fraud Order stick. The boy was just out of the Navy, though, and he didn't feel like fighting the government, no matter how much in the wrong it might be. Besides, he planned to go back to College, so he felt that he might as well drop the business entirely and get back to his books.

Unless you are a lawyer, the chances are that you would have felt the same way about it, for few people starting in the mail order business have the money or the inclination to take on a lawsuit, especially against the Post Office. Most will do anything in reason to avoid it.

And there are three ways in which the above offers can be used, we believe, without running foul of any Post Office prejudices. Here they are:

1. Keep circulation local and instead of enclosing an order form, have your customers come to your office or store and buy your products over the counter. It is only when money is sent through the mails that the Post Office has jurisdiction.

2. Hire canvassers on a commission basis to sell your product door to door. Here again the money is paid over in person and the Post Office has no jurisdiction.

3. We are not quite so sure of this method, but we do know that it has been used by one concern for ten years without interference by the Post Office. That is to confine your circularizing to your own state. You will then be doing an intra-state business, and most government bureaus will have no jurisdiction over you. We believe that applies to the Post Office, too, and all the lawyers we have consulted agree with us, though they are not certain on this point.

If you would like to use the afore-mentioned letter and circular in one of the three ways outlined above, you can get the B-Kelp in wholesale quantities of 48 bottles to the carton (each bottle containing 100 tablets one month's supply) from St. George's Fellowship, 646 Fernando Bldg., 406 South Main St., Los Angeles, California, at a discount of 70% from the retail price of $3.00 a bottle.

You will have to be just as careful in selling vitamins or anything else that can be regarded as self-medication as you would in selling B-Kelp. Even beauty preparations such as face creams and the like may bring you into conflict with some government bureau, for the New Deal has given us a bureaucracy almost as powerful and all-inclusive as that of Stalin or Hitler. For those who would like to test out some home-made beauty cream, however, here is a letter that night readily adapted to its sale:

* * *

Now Science Explains What Causes Face 'Wrinkles'.
Even Older Women Can Have Soft, Lovely, Velvety Skin!

Dear Madam:

"How can I make myself more beautiful?"

How often have you asked yourself that question? And what has been the answer? Hasn't it been, "By finding some way to restore the softness and youthful loveliness of my skin?"

No matter how fine your features, you cannot have real beauty without a fresh, healthy skin. And now, at last, science gives you the secret. Like all great discoveries, it is simple. It can be given you in seven words.

RESTORE TO YOUR SKIN
ITS NATURAL OILS
And its youthful freshness and beauty
will promptly return

Does that sound too simple? Well, just ask yourself, "What is it that makes the skin of the face and neck dry and wrinkled?" NOT age. Look at the skin on other parts of your body. It is youthful and fresh as when you were a babe. Yet it is as old in years as the skin of your face. What then makes the difference?

STARVATION, that *is what does it!* Between wind and sun and flying particles of dust, and the lye and soda of strong soaps, the natural oils of your face and neck have not a chance. They have dried out until the cells of your skin are starved. Pores are clogged so they no longer function. Your skin is OLD, dried out before its time, like the arteries of some old man.

Science has shown you know, that age is not a matter of years. Biologically, there is no reason why one must grow old. Men age and dry up because they do not throw off the waste products fast enough. Arteries become clogged. Poisons and waste harden inside them, stepping up the pores, making it impossible to get the necessary nourishment through to the cells. Result? A gradual starving and drying up of the cells.

Well, that is just what has been happening to the skin of your face. The cells have been drying up for lack of proper nourishment. The pores through which they breathe have become clogged. Naturally your cheeks will sag under those conditions. Naturally the skin will develop scores of tiny lines and wrinkles.

The remedy? There are only two:

1. Help the pores throw off the dust and dried skin that is clogging them, and thus enable the nourishment to get to your skin cells from within.

2. Replenish the natural oils of the skin from the outside, through the use of a youthifying crème made up only of vital active oils, with no waxes, mineral oils or grease as a base.

Simple things, both of these; opening the pores so your starved skin cells can breathe again and draw upon the blood stream for nourishment, and renewing the flow of natural oils by replenishing them from without. Yet that is where "Lotus-Creme" can be a real Fountain of Youth for you.

You see, "Lotus-Creme" is a soft, golden white, penetrating crème composed exclusively of vital, active oils. Its function is to stimulate the skin by replacing natural deficiencies. Compounded of ingredients approved by skin specialists and physicians, it contains a special vital oil that penetrates to the sub-epidermal layers of the skin, nourishes them and enables them to rebuild the soft, glowing skin of youth.

"Lotus-Creme" depends for its results—not upon magic or harsh astringents or the like—but upon

Nature herself. Since the first dawn of created life, Nature has nourished every form of cell life by absorption. It surrounds them with the elements they need for life and growth, and lets the cells absorb them.

That is exactly what happens when you rub "Lotus-Creme" into your skin. You are surrounding every tiny cell with the life-giving elements from vital, active oils—NOT choking them with waxes, greases and other inert elements. There is nothing about "Lotus-Creme" to stick in the pores, to clog them as do many ordinary creams. That is why it so truly rejuvenates the skin. That is why the results are apparent so quickly.

"Lotus-Creme" actually feeds these hungry skin cells, helps them fill out, grow young and firm again. As you massage it into your starved skin, you can almost feel the years roll back. Certainly, you will notice the difference from day to day in your mirror, as it magically irons out those tiny, tell-tale lines and wrinkles.

Would you risk $1.00 for such an Elixir of Youth? Would you pay that much for the chance to TRY one of the few preparations known to cosmetologists that really penetrates the true skin and nourishes it in a natural way?

Mind you, the $1.00 you send will not be ours until you have used the special jar of "Lotus-Creme" for 30 days, and are SATISFIED that it will do everything we claim for it. You can have the $1.00 back at any time within the 30 days, merely by returning the empty jar.

On that distinct understanding, would you risk $1.00 for the Secret of a Youthful Skin? If you would, then use the enclosed Coupon. It will bring you (if *mailed at once*) our regular $1.50 jar of "Lotus-Creme" for a month's trial, at the special introductory price of $1.00. It will bring you this 3 oz. jar, postpaid, with full directions as to how to care for the face without drying its natural oils, how to nourish the skin, how to regain beauty that need never fade.

But, it will bring you a jar of "Lotus-Creme" at the special Introductory Price of $1.00 *only if you mail the Coupon at once.* This is a Trial Offer; good for ten days only. If a soft, alluring, rejuvenated skin is worth $1.00 to you, then send the enclosed Coupon NOW. You may never have another chance.

Sincerely,

* * *

The one thing all men are more interested in than anything else is themselves. They buy health books and health products because they want to feel better, to look better, and to get more out of life.

And if you can make them feel more important through other products, they will buy these, too. Here are two letters offering letter heads that have been used with unusual success.

* * *

Is Your Name and Address, As Given,
On the Enclosed Card, CORRECT?

Dear Friend:

I am going to send to you, in the next few days, a Deluxe box of fine social stationery, with your three-letter Monogram beautifully imprinted on it. There will be 50 sheets of note-head paper of amazingly fine quality, bearing your monogram at the top and 50 envelopes to match.

Before I send it, however, I want to make sure that I have your initials correct. Will you check them on the enclosed card, please, and return it to me?

In our fathers' day, you know, no one of your social standing would have thought of writing personal notes on other than engraved letterheads. Today monogrammed noteheads and envelopes beautifully imprinted on Deluxe paper are even more distinctive and personal than the engraved ones of olden times.

You see, artistically designed monograms are more decorative than the cold and lifeless engraving. They add such life and distinction that they have come to be regarded as the accepted form for social correspondence. I have made up a special box for you this year, largely to introduce to you and other old customers our new Deluxe Monogrammed stationary. It contains 50 Monogrammed Note-heads with envelopes to match, on fine quality letter paper.

The price? You'll smile when you hear it. Only $1.00 post-paid. You'd probably pay twice that for them elsewhere, if you COULD buy them in stores.

Folks from all over the country have written me in previous years to say: "Gorgeous!" "Haven't seen anything to equal them in Gift Shops." "Don't see how you can sell such goods at your low price." Just wait until they see this year's box. It is far superior even to what we have offered in the past that they are going to be hard put to it to find superlatives to describe it.

You see, we make up these special assortments each year for Direct-by-Mail sales to a selected group of discriminating buyers, thus doing away with store profit and allowing us to set a price that is extremely LOW.

Not only that, but we send them to you at our own risk and expense for a WEEK'S FREE EXAMINATION!

Send no money. Just your name and address on the enclosed card will bring you this beautiful new box without cost and without obligation. You can examine it, compare it with anything you can find in stores, then return it at our expense if you are not more than pleased.

On that understanding, will you TRY it? And will you mark your initials on the card, just as you want them to appear on that deluxe stationery?

Sincerely,

* * *

The Top Two Inches Of Your Letterhead
Is The Cheapest Advertising Space You Can Buy!

Dear Reader:

I was going to write you a long letter, telling you why you ought to use a letterhead that will give people a good impression of you and of your social and business standing—how much first impressions grow into confidence. and confidence into friendliness and regard.

But what's the use?

You know that as well as I could tell you. You know that your letterhead has as much significance to the person reading your letter as your own appearance has to the man you call upon. And you know that the top two inches of your letterhead, the part where your name and address appear, is just as important in creating a favorable impression as the coat and collar and tie you wear.

The point is this; I have studied personal stationery so long, and handled so much of it, that I know how to give it all the prestige and power that is possible to put into type, backed by fine quality paper.

I want your order, because I know that I can give you a really worth-while value for your money. The price? It costs no more to do good work than the ordinary kind. You pay only the usual charge of $4.95 for 250 Monarch size letterheads, 7 ¼" x 10½", printed on fine rag paper, with 250 envelopes to match with your name and address on the flap.

You pay your $4.95 for the workmanship and fine rag paper. The greatest value you get FREE. That is the judgment acquired from long years of experience in handling thousands upon thousands of such orders. You'd have paid me the same $4.95 ten years ago for just the workmanship and paper. You'd have gotten perhaps better than an ordinary job, certainly as good value as any other printer could give you, but today I give you twice that value, twice that intangible something—quality, prestige, atmosphere.

Will you TRY me? Just letter your name and address on the enclosed form in the way you want them to be printed. Then sit back and watch the results.

Sincerely,

* * *

Most people in business or thinking of going into business want to raise money. If they are already in business, they are sure to have some delinquent accounts that they would like to know how to collect. Here is a letter that supplies the answer to their heart's desire. It gives them some of the most successful collection letters ever used. It shows them how to raise money. This letter was used by George H. Cole, State Tower Bldg., Syracuse, New York We understand that Mr. Cole is willing to make a satisfactory wholesale price to any who wish to sell his course by mail.

* * *

Want to raise money?
While they last, the famous *"Notes on Financing"*
FREE

Gentlemen:

Would you like to see bigger and better collections

in a few short weeks? Let me tell you how.

I am going to send within the next few days a choice collection of marvelous letters—the cream of the very best collection letters ever written.

These letters are probably not like any you have ever seen before, because:

1. They actually are the "pick" of the most effective collection letters ever used—and especially valuable right now.

2. They are the ones which have produced the best results ever attained in actual use.

3. All are friendly, Courteous preserving and often creating good will.

4. They substitute experience for experiment and are suitable to any business without revision.

I am going to send these wonder letters with no obligation on your part, for you to read and ACTUALLY TRY OUT at my risk and expense.

But there's just one thing, I don't want to send them without first getting your permission. You can grant that in a moment by Penciling the Courtesy Card enclosed.

When I said the letters, there's absolutely no obligation to keep them. While I want you to know first hand the great results they will obtain in actual use—you are perfectly free to return them for any reason or for no reason at all.

But here's the most important part:

If you find they are everything I say about them and you are to be the sole judge—how much would you expect to pay for them? *$25.00? $50.00? $100.00?* That's what they will be worth to you based on actual RESULTS they'll get for you. Use them side by side with those you are now using and compare results! Certainly if they will do half of what I've promised you they would be worth that and more.

Well, if you decide to try out these letters, you need send me, not $25.00, or $50.00, or even the regular price of $10.00; but MY SPECIAL INTRODUCTORY PRICE TO YOU of $3.85.

And that isn't all. If within three months your $3.85 hasn't grown to many times that amount in collections made and good-will preserved, send back the letters and I'll refund to you cheerfully and in full every cent you have paid for them.

Remember there are no strings of any kind to my offer. If within just three months they haven't helped you to the pot of gold at the end of the rainbow by collecting many, many times their cost, then they are not for you. Send them back and get your money.

And I want you to note this:

These wonder letters are by no means an ordinary "series." They are not a series of threats or ordinary "dunning" letters. Nor are they the familiar "tear out forms." They're the aristocrats of the collection field.

And just listen to this:

"The letters are the work of geniuses—and worth thousands of dollars." So writes Charles Hardman of Chicago.

For they are the best of the best—and gotten together, I assure you, only after the expenditure of much time and effort.

The Famous *"Notes on Financing"* Free

And for good measure (while they last) I'll send you the very unusual and practical *"Notes on Financing the Business of Moderate Size,"* with my compliments, at no cost whatever. You'll find them interesting and very valuable if you ever want to raise money for your business.

But you'll have to send the Courtesy Card right away, for we're running off only a limited number of sets for this Advance Edition. And advanced orders are coming in so fast that I'm afraid all of them will be spoken for very quickly.

So if you want these WONDER LETTERS without risk of loss and the NOTES ON FINANCING free, you'll have to mail the Courtesy Card, NOW—TODAY.

Yours for better business,

* * *

Any original and unique idea can oftentimes be developed into a successful mail order business. I came across one a short time ago which offers a special wax for taking the "saw-edge" off stiff collars Surprisingly enough, it has been built into a profitable business.

A man in Pennsylvania had an idea for a metal desk file. He kept adding improvements to it until he had an unusual and worth while article. Then he sent out the following letter, and with it he sold more than a hundred thousand of those files.

* * *

Dear Sir:

Two years ago I set about to develop a handy, metal, full-size letter file for the top of my desk. a place where I could keep in good order my personal letters, bills, receipts, tax records, insurance records and other things of a private nature.

Before I was through, that special Personal File had cost over $50.00. I wouldn't have sold it for $100. But I've since had this Personal File produced in quantities (exactly like my own original model) and can offer them for only $6.95.

You may get some idea of how remarkable and valuable this Personal File really is when I tell you that more than 33,000 men have since ordered one from me for use in Office, home or for gifts. You may get some idea of how it increases personal efficiency, when I tell you that I have received the most enthusiastic letters of thanks one ever read, from a great many of the 33,000 who have bought this Personal File.

A busy United States Congressman took time to

write from Washington while Congress was actually in session, "It is just what I have been looking for, for a long time. It suits me exactly." A Houston business man says,

"Its value is ten times the price I paid." And a prominent Baltimore professional man exclaims, "It is worth its weight in gold."

THE INTERESTING HISTORY OF THE PERSONAL FILE

When the Personal File was first born, it was just a simple box of strong steel, the right height and width to take full-size business letters, (the right depth for 1,000 of them) with a complete filing system of heavy cardboard folders inside, a hinged lid with sturdy lock, the File neatly finished in baked enamel just like other fine office equipment. It looked something like this "typewritten picture." (Picture here.)

I was tickled pink with the way it served my needs. But I used it so much that, as it became nearly full, it was harder to file and find the papers I wanted, So I had the front changed to a sliding, expanding front which made it easy as pie to file or find any paper even when the File was filled to capacity. The expanding front made the File like this . . . (Picture here.)

After awhile, I realized that there were certain extra-personal things (copy of my Will was one of them) which I wanted to keep under lock and key at all times—yet I wanted my Stenographer to have access to the main part of the File. So I conceived the idea of putting another hinged door on the *inside* of the lids, making a "secret compartment" under separate lock and key. Like this . . . (Picture here.)

Lastly, I made some other refinements and additions—putting a staunch handle on the top so my Personal File could be carried between Office and Home, or to a meeting—adding a metal frame on the front in which I inserted my personal card—putting felt pads on the bottom to protect my desk. Now I think my Personal File is beyond improvement. And so do the other 33,000 users, judging from the letters I receive almost every day.

WILL YOU TRY THIS PERSONAL FILE FOR A WEEK—FREE?

This Personal File is too unique to describe with words. It is too valuable and would have too important an effect on the way you'd conduct your affairs, for me to explain. You have to see it, try it, use it for a few days to really appreciate its almost human helpfulness.

If you will merely mail the enclosed Free Trial Card, I'll send you one, by Prepaid Parcel Post, for a WEEK'S FREE TRIAL. If you are willing to part with this Personal File after you've had it for a week, return it at my expense. The trial will not have cost you a single penny.

If you agree with the 33,000 users of this Personal File, if you decide you want to hire it to help keep your personal things in order, for the rest of your life, send only $6.95 as payment in full.

This low price of $6.95 is made possible only through the economies of huge quantity production, and selling them directly-by-mail. If this Personal File were made only a few hundred at a time, and sold through jobbers, Salesmen and Dealers, I believe they'd have to sell for $12.00 at least. Maybe $15.00!

But do not delay! Steel, locks, filing equipment, labor, everything has gone up sharply and is still going up. The Personal Files now on hand were made some time ago, and the $6.95 price is based on costs at that time. When these are gone, the $6.95 price will probably be gone, too. So mail the Free Trial Card AT ONCE, while I can guarantee the low price!

Yours for Convenience and Privacy,

* * *

"The Postage Stamp" of March, 1947, had an interesting article about just such a mail order venture. We quote it.

"There is inspiration in the life of Parker B. Fiske, who died recently. A successful engineer, he became paralyzed in one arm and a leg. Flat on his back and down to his last $4.41, his future looked like a blank wall painted black.

"A lesser man would have pined away his days, cursing his dire fate. Not Parker B. Fiske. In his darkest hours, the flame of an unquenchable spirit burned on.

"He sparked an idea —FIRE MAGIC— a wax mixed with chemicals that burned with rainbow flames in the home hearth, to heighten the color of fireside dreams.

"From his bed, Parker B. projected his glowing personality by mail to Suppliers and dealers and inside of ten years, ran his $4.41 up to a $200,000 yearly volume by the magic of his FIRE MAGIC. In his head he desired production machinery he was never to see for the efficient manufacture of his product he built and managed the factory he never set foot in. Most of his clients never knew that the man they dealt with was not an ordinary business man operating in the usual way.

"There is inspiration in the life of Parker B. Fiske."

Not all of us have original ideas, and for those who have not, the easiest product on which to start a small mail order business is probably one related to health. In this connection we give you below a letter that has never been used, but which we believe will sell even better than the one on B-Kelp, because the product it offers is just as rich in food iodine, yet sells for only $1.00 instead of $3.00.

This product is MARINEX You can get it in wholesale quantities of 48 bottles to the carton at a price of 30 cents a bottle. Just send to George's Fellowship, 646 Fernando Bldg., 406 South Main St., Los Angeles, California.

The letter offers the same little book that was sold in connection with *Nature's Own Deterrent to Old Age.* This is a book you can get at 20 cents a copy by sending to Income Builders, West 42nd St., New York, New York 18.

Adding 20 cents for the booklet to the cost of a bottle of Marinex makes a total of 50 cents. That brings the cost of your product up pretty high. You probably will not make money on your first sale. But remember your first sale is like the first Olive out of the bottle; all the rest come easier for it. This booklet sells your customer on his need of Food Iodine, and should do more to make him a permanent customer, ordering your product month after month, than anything you could tell him. So even if you LOSE money on your first sale of Marinex, we believe it will be a Worthwhile investment.

Here is the letter:

* * *

May We Send You, With Our Compliments,
A Month's *Supply Of MARINEX, Rich in Food Iodine?*

Dear Customer:

"Old Age" is a disease - the effect of intoxications and inactions. It must come to all of us some time, of course ... *but that time can be put off!*

It has been found, for instance that the USEFUL life of a cow may be increased from the average of five years, to seven eight years.

Now their experiments have led a number of English Scientists to believe that the USEFUL life of man may be increased by perhaps 20 to 25 years!

Dr. W. Mitchell Stevens, one of Britain's great medical authorities, wrote a book and many articles in scientific journals telling how to assist man's natural resistance to "Old Age" and disease by ensuring that the natural defenses are maintained at their maximum potency at any age and under any circumstances.

He wrote, "In my opinion, the role played by IODINE in fortifying the natural defenses will one day be accepted. IODINE . . . is of infinitely greater importance as a *natural activator of defense substances.*"

He went on to suggest its use by all people over 40

years of age to ensure the maximum duration of life, and here is his conclusion.

"I feel confident that an extensive experimenting by clinicians with the natural element IODINE will, by the prevention and treatment of disease in its broadest sense, do more for the maintenance of health and the extension of USEFUL life than will any combination of physiologists, pathologists, etc., working in laboratories."

Other authorities write in similar vein. Harry R. Litchfield in the *Medical Record,* wrote, "IODINE should be added to our daily ration in the same manner as we add Vitamin D to milk and bread. It promotes efficient mental development; an inadequate supply before birth may even produce anything from imbecility to mere mental dullness."

Of all the glands in your body, the most important is the THYROID, for it guides and to an extent regulates all the other glands. In his article, Litchfield had this to say about the Thyroid.

"Recent research by Bauman and Kendall established the fact that IODINE furnishes the most important element which enables the thyroid gland to produce Thyroxin, which hormone regulates the basal metabolic rate and determines the rate of function of all the glands in the body."

Without IODINE, your Thyroid gland would not function. And without a properly functioning Thyroid, you would quickly develop old age weaknesses and other ailments.

Yet IODINE is largely lacking in many of the foods you eat, especially in certain large sections of the country. It is only the sea foods that are rich in it.

U. S. Government reports set forth the minimum daily human need for Iodine as 100 grams, but considerably more than that would seem to be desirable when the system has long been starved of Iodine.

Beef, potatoes, eggs, contain tiny amounts of IODINE. Salt water fish considerably more. But where even the best fish contain less than 300 parts of IODINE to the billion, vegetables from the floor of the sea, like Pacific Sea Kelp of which MARINEX is made, contain 900,000!

A few tablets daily made of pure, dehydrated Pacific Sea Kelp, will assure you of an abundant supply of vital FOOD IODINE, and if you mail the enclosed Gift Coupon at once, you will get a full month's supply of MARINEX, *with our compliments!*

Over in England, where the food problem is so acute, scientists have been experimenting with Food Iodine for many years, and some of their discoveries are startling in the extreme. In a little book called,

"IODINE:
Nature's Own Deterrent To Old Age"

The findings of leading scientists of Britain and the world have been brought together, showing the results that have been obtained through the use of

FOOD IODINE. Not only do they regard FOOD IODINE as the element that combats "Old Age" and its attendant ills, not only do they look upon it as the only factor that will prevent goiter, but they believe that mental growth, normal weight and resistance to disease are just a few of the other benefits that may come from its use.

The price of "*IODINE—Nature's Own Deterrent to Old Age*" is only $1.00. It is a small book, and may not from the outside look to be worth even that low price, but when you have read it you will agree that the facts it gives you would be cheap at many times the price.

But that isn't all. With this little book, you get a full month's supply of MARINEX (regularly priced at $1.00), *with our compliments.* Try it for 30 days. If you are not more than pleased, return the book and your $1.00 will be refunded a full at once.

You won't get results overnight, of course. Natural, organic FOOD IODINE is not a medicine. It is altogether different from medicinal iodine. Natural, organic FOOD IODINE is a food supplement, and it is one that is vitally necessary to the proper functioning of your thyroid gland.

Naturally the results will not be apparent at once. Dr. Stevens reported the experience of three other doctors, all 58 years old or over who tried Iodine on themselves, in different forms. The first said it had a wonderful effect upon him; the second wrote that he had never been in better health; the third reported his general health much improved, and that he felt younger (and his friends told him he looked younger) than for five years.

We don't guarantee that it will have the same effect on you, of course, because other factors may be involved besides lack of IODINE. But we do promise you that if you are not more than satisfied with the results, you have only to return the little book and we will refund your $1.00 without question.

On that understanding, will you mail the enclosed Gift coupon? TODAY?

Sincerely,

* * *

St. George's Fellowship has a number of other vitamins and mineral products that they will sell readily to anyone who first buys B-Kelp or Marinex, or that you could use as your original offer. Here is a list of them with the retail and wholesale prices (quantities of 48 or more).

	Retail	Wholesale
Garlic Parsley (High Blood Pressure)	$1.50	.45
Calcium and Vegetable Tabs (Rich in Calcium, Plant Iron)	$1.00	.30
Vitergex (Nerve Nourishment, "Brain-Fog")	$1.00	.40
Organic Iodine Tabs (Gland Disorders)	$1.00	.30
Vitamin B Complex (Appetite, Digestion, Nutrition)	$2.00	.60
Vitamin C (Bleeding gums, Anemia, Anti-Infection)	$2.00	.60

Cal-Di (Calcium, Phosphorous, Vita. D. Iron, "Blood-Building")	$2.00	.60
Chlor-a-veg (Vita A and Chlorophyll for Colds, Sinus)	$3.00	.70
B-Kelp	$3.00	.70

With such a start, you will be on your way to the building of a profitable spare time business, which can grow and keep you in comfort for the rest of your days. In the remaining five lessons, you will find their products and other methods. You can try any of them on this customer list of yours, for the important thing to remember is that the most valuable asset any mail order business can have is its list of customers… the people who know you and believe in you and will ay from you almost anything you may offer them.

Get a few thousand such customers who buy something from you each month, and you will have a business that should keep you in comfort and luxuries the rest of your days.

LESSON III

START WITH WHAT YOU HAVE

There is a famous Church in one of the big Eastern cities, costing more than $100,000 to build, that was started on an initial capital of only 57 cents.

Its congregation was small and poor, consisting for the most part of working men and women, so there seemed little chance of raising money for a new church, when the structure they were using got too small for their needs.

The quarters there were so meager, however, that at the services each Sunday a number of people had to stand, so one poor little girl, who couldn't get even a seat in Sunday School, decided to save her pennies to help build a larger church.

A few months later she was taken sick and died, but while she lay on her death-bed, she asked for her bank and when it was brought to her, she begged her mother to take the money to the minister as a start towards a new church. There were only 57 pennies in the bank, and 57 cents seemed such a ridiculously small amount compared to the cost of a modern building that the mother was reluctant to offer them, but the child insisted, so she promised.

It happened that on the following Sunday, when she gave the money to the minister with the child's message, the Lesson was from the parable of the loaves and fishes. The minister had been inclined to smile at the idea of accepting 57 cents as the start of a building fund, but when he read the Lesson, it came to him that if Jesus could feed 5,000 people with five barley loaves and two fishes, he could just as readily build a church with only 57 cents.

So the minister took the 57 pennies, blessed them, and gave them out as Jesus had done, gave them to his congregation to use as seeds for the money they would need for their new building. How those seeds increased and multiplied makes a story in itself. A poor congregation, without a large membership or rich families to help, they built a wonderful church costing well over $100,000, and *all on an initial capital of* 57 cents!

Not only that, but the whole congregation seemed to prosper, seemed to be freer from sickness, seemed to be happier in every way.

And all because they didn't wait for fortune to come to *them, they started with, what they had!*

Plenty of people will tell you that if only they had money, they would build orphanages, they would endow charitable institutions, they would help the world in every way. But how many have the courage to start with 57cents?

George Muller did it. A poor man, he saw orphans neglected, near to starvation. So he used what little he had to help them. Strange to say, that little, instead of being quickly gone, seemed to grow! Like the widow's measure of meal and cruse of oil, there seemed to be an inexhaustible supply behind it. Muller built and maintained five orphanages; he spent more than $5,000,000, and all without any visible means of supply!

It is like the story of St. Teresa. The need for places of refuge in her day was vastly greater than now, so Teresa too conceived the idea of an orphanage. Broaching the matter to her superiors, she was asked how much money she had. "Three ducats!" was her answer. They laughed at her. Build an orphanage with three ducats? The woman must be crazy.

"It is true," she told them calmly, "that with only Teresa and three ducats, I can do little. But with God and Teresa and three ducats, I can do anything!" And with those three ducats for a start, St. Teresa built an orphanage and performed a work that made her famous.

She had the courage to start with what she had. As in the poem by Walter Filkin:

"They shook their wise heads as some others had done;
They shouted that no one could do it;
They settled the thing and the task was begun;
It couldn't be done and they knew it.
Right then came a lad most determined and strong;
If doubt dwelt within he soon hid it;
His face was a star; in his soul was song;
He rolled up his sleeves and he did it!"

To tell you that with a dollar or two you can start a business that may grow so big that it will keep you and your family all your days, may sound silly. Yet it has been done repeatedly, and what has been done once can be done again.

Back in 1929, for instance, when everyone was in the "dumps," when millions had lost their last cent and the bottom seemed to have dropped out of everything, Frank B. Robinson of Moscow, Idaho, got the idea for a course of lessons that should show people how to meet the seemingly insurmountable obstacles that were surrounding them on all sides, how to use them as stepping-stones to success.

Robinson was only a drug clerk in the local pharmacy at the time. He had a wife and two children, and a lot of debts, and the most cash he could lay his hands on was only $40. So most people in his circumstances, would have sighed and bemoaned the fact that a poor man has no chance, and put his idea in cold storage pending the time when some rich angel would come around to finance it.

Not so Frank B. Robinson. He decided that if his idea was good, the time to start it was right then, and the way to begin was to START.

So he took part of his $40 to a printer and got him to print a few hundred copies of a sales letter describing his course, together with order forms, envelopes and descriptive matter.

Then he sent to a number of newspapers a small ad to be inserted in the PERSONAL column of the Classified Advertising section. Because I cannot well reproduce Robinson's own ads here, I give you below a classified ad that Income Builders used on a booklet of our own. These booklets, and the Course it advertised, were handled in exactly the same way as Robinson's Course, so I give you below the copy and the methods used.

* * *

GOD NEVER ORDERED IT THUS

Why should we be hard up, debt-ridden, worried or distressed? In this world there is plenty for all if we will only use the Fundamental Law of Increase, the law that tells you how to have your share of the good things of life.

Send for FREE inspiring 16-page book that tells you about using this law as a way to success. Your name on a penny post-card will bring your copy FREE. Income Builders, Dept. 56-D, 152 West 42nd Street, New York, New York

* * *

First we inserted this 11-line ad in the "Personal" columns of the Classified Advertising Sections of such newspapers as the *Philadelphia Inquirer*, the *New York News, New York Mirror, Los Angeles Examiner, Indianapolis Star, Denver Post*, etc. The cost varies from 20 cents a line to 50 cents or 75 cents a line, depending upon the circulation of the paper. The *New York News* and *Mirror* have out-of-town editions at special rates that enable you to test any new project or idea on a wide cross-section of the newspaper reading public at a cost of only 50 cents to 65 cents a line, and it is surprising how much of a "hook" you can put into three or four lines of copy, getting your reader's attention and impelling him to send for your booklet or circular giving more information.

From the 11-line ads that Income Builders put in the newspapers, they got responses at an average cost of about 7 cents per inquiry.

To those who wrote asking for copy of the free booklet, Income Builders sent a copy of the booklet called *"God Never Ordered It Thus,"* and with it, the following letter:

* * *

Dear Mr. Jones:

The 16-page booklet you sent for, *"God Never Ordered It Thus"*, is enclosed. It is a pleasure to send it to you, with our compliments

If you have ever been in a laboratory, and watched a live cell under a microscope, you know how all cell life increases. It first divides, each part grows back to the size of the original cell, then each divides again, and so on. That is the principle of growth used throughout all of Nature, — "DIVIDE, and GROW!" It is the only principle of INCREASE known to man.

As you will see in the booklet enclosed, you can go back over all the miracles of increase told in the Bible, and every one uses that same principle. We call them "miracles" but they are really demonstrations of NATURAL LAW, a Law that works as surely today as ever it did in the days of Jesus or the Prophets.

What was the real mission of Jesus? Did He ever say we had to be poor or suffer or be miserable in order to win peace and contentment and happiness here and hereafter? No, indeed. That is merely what some orthodox religions teach. "I came," Jesus said, "that ye might have LIFE, and have it more ABUNDANTLY."

And again and again He demonstrated abundance—at the marriage feast when He turned water into wine, in the desert when He increased the loaves and fishes, at the seaside when He filled the Apostles' nets with fish. Far from being the "Man of Sorrows" that so many picture Him, He was the center of JOY wherever He went, children flocked to Him, He was the most sought after dinner guest in Jerusalem. So much so that the solemn, long-faced Scribes and Pharisees accused Him of consorting only with publicans and sinners.

Go back over all the promises of the Scriptures, both the Old and the New Testament and you will find that they are promises of abundance NOW! All are contingent upon your complying with certain laws, but when you do your part, you are to get the reward NOT in some dim and distant hereafter, but NOW, right here on earth.

The Law of Life is INCREASE. Go through all of Nature, and you find that everything alive is constantly dividing and growing. So you can have whatever you want, IF YOU PLANT IT! You can harvest any good thing you wish if *you will but sow the seed!* Remember it was Jesus who said, "By their fruits ye shall know them." You were not born to be poor or unhappy or unwell. You were born to inherit the earth!

But before you can win that inheritance, you must learn the Law of Increase, and just how it works. Ever since he wrote, *"The Secret of the Ages,"* which sold over 300,000 sets and is quoted the world over, Robert Collier has been working on a course of 24 Lessons which should show to every reader the Fundamental Law of all life as it is related to the problem of increase.

So fundamental is this Law that you can prove it for yourself by watching how it works in physics, in electro-mechanics, in surgery and in all of Nature. You can see it work in your own life, watch it make your own career NOT in some dim and distant future, but now, TODAY, Anno Domini 1947.

I know a man who had not a cent to his name nor food enough in the house for another meal for his wife and three children, when this Law was brought home to him and through it he made a fortune. A similar story is that of Charles Page, whose amazing experience was written up in the *American Magazine* some time ago. Then there was George Mueller, who raised some five millions from nothing. And Vashni Young, who afterwards wrote *"A Fortune to Share."* I could tell you of dozens who were hopelessly in debt, some who were sick, some sunk in despair, yet by contacting this law, every one won through, some to fame, fortune and honors, all to contentment and happiness.

Mind you, it was not from us that this knowledge came to them. But they did learn the working of the law, and out of that knowledge came good to them.

For ten years now, Robert Collier has been studying this Law and how it works. For ten years he has been writing a Course of 24 Lessons showing clearly and unmistakably how to use the Law to win success. And a couple of years ago, he made ready to publish this Course.

His first pre-publication price was $28, but people wrote asking why he could not put it up in less expensive form and sell it at a figure within easy reach of all, so he took the most important essentials from all the 24 Lessons, re-wrote them in short, readable form, and put them into seven brief, meaty lessons.

To those who will mail the enclosed reservation right away, I am going to send these seven Lessons NOT at $28, BUT FOR LESS THAN A FIFTH OF THAT PRICE, only $4.85!

Mind you, these seven Lessons contain all the ESSENTIALS, the real meat, of the originally planned 24-Lesson Course. There is not as much explanation, and no unnecessary detail, but everything USABLE is there in a form you can readily understand and put into immediate practice.

Will you TRY these seven meaty Lessons, if I send them to you subject to 30 days' examination, to be returned and your $4.85 refunded in full if you are not more than satisfied? Will you read them; put them to the test, watch them work in your life and your career?

Remember, you not only have 30 days in which to examine and try them before we regard it as a sale, but even after the 30 days are up, you get this additional guarantee.

If within six months your $4.85 has not brought you at least $300 of ADDITIONAL EARNINGS, send back the Lessons and I'll refund to you cheerfully and in full *every cent you have paid to me for them!*

There are no conditions, no strings of any kind to this offer. If within six months these Lessons have not shown you how to use the Law of Increase to bring you what you want, then they are not for you. Send them back and get your money!

So don't decide about buying now. You can do that later. Send me now only the Reservation enclosed, with your name and address on it. Then, AFTER the 30 days are up, AFTER you have put the Law of Increase to the test, you can decide whether or not you want to keep the Lessons. If you decide to return them, I'll pay the charges both ways.

But it is important that you send the Reservation right away, for I printed a special Gift Edition for the Holidays, very attractively done, and I have only a comparatively few of this left. If your order comes while we still have copies of this Gift Edition, I will have one personally inscribed to you and AUTOGRAPHED by the Author.

So if you want to try out your hidden powers without cost and without obligation, mail the enclosed Reservation NOW— while it is in your hand—before anything comes along to make you forget it.

Yours, for DREAMS COME TRUE

INCOME BUILDERS

* * *

That was the first letter. It brought back about 15% to 20% of orders, which was good, because with 100 inquiries having cost approximately $7.00, and 100 letters and booklets in the mail costing $40.00 more, Income Builders got back more than its selling cost from the first 15 orders at $4.95—$72.75. If you can get 15% from your first sales letter you can feel reasonably sure of more than doubling that with two or three follow-ups.

Below is the second letter we used on these inquiries. It pulled close to 8% of orders and thus definitely put the effort in the profit column.

* * *

Use This Prosperity Law In Your Affairs.
Have You Ever Noticed the Striking Similarity of. . .

*The Great Prosperity Demonstrations
In The Bible?*

Dear Customer:

Would you like to get a more interesting job, have more money to spend for the luxuries as well as the necessities of life?

Let me tell you a way:

Nearly 2,000 years ago, there came to this earth a Man who proclaimed that His mission was to show us a more ABUNDANT life. He turned water into wine. He fed thousands with only five loaves and two fishes, yet had twelve basketfuls left. He brought forth gold from a fish's mouth. And all the things He did, *He assured us that we could do also!*

If these were the only cases of sudden increase known to man, they might be regarded as "miracles" and impossible to ordinary mortals like ourselves. But go back over the Scriptural writings, and you find the records of others. There is the widow of Zarephath, who fed Elijah for many days, and had plenty left for herself and her son, though she started with only a measure of meal and a little oil sufficient for one meal. There is the case of the widow who went to Elisha to save her son from bondage. There are other cases in the Scriptural writings, and every man has read of modern experiences almost as "miraculous."

Now the peculiar thing about every instance of this kind is that they all conform to one fundamental, natural *law—the Law of Division and Growth.* Take every form of cell life, on land or sea, in humans, plants, or animals, and the same principle applies. From the beginning of time, the only method of increase known to Nature has been— *"Divide. . .,* and GROW."

You see, Nature is logical in all that she does. She makes no exceptions. She plays no favorites. Learn her formulas and you get results consistently. Remain ignorant of them, and you get what you want haphazardly or not at all.

The important thing to remember about the miracles of Jesus is the fact that He was not making use of some special power that He alone possessed, else would He never have told us to "Go and do in like manner," or that "The things that He did, could we do also, and greater things than these could we do." He was the "Way-shower." *He was showing us how* to *use the Law of Increase, a* law that always has worked and always will work for those who learn how to use it.

> *You* can use this Law to increase YOUR prosperity just as the Master, used it to supply food for the hungry multitudes, or money for the tax collectors.

But before trying to use it, it is well to learn just what the Law is and how it works. Ever since he wrote *"The Secret of the Ages"* (which sold over 300,000 sets and is quoted the world over) Robert Collier has been working on a Course of 24 Lessons which should show to every reader the Fundamental Law of all Life as it is related to the problem of increase.

So fundamental is this Law that you can prove it for yourself by watching how it works in physics, in electro-mechanics in surgery and in all of Nature. You can see it work in your own life; watch it make your own career, NOT in some dim and distant future, but now, TODAY, Anno Domini 1947!

I know a man who had not a cent to his name nor food enough in the house for another meal for his wife and three children, when this Law was brought home to him — and through it he made a fortune. A similar story is that of Charles Page, whose amazing experience was written up in the *American Magazine* some time ago. Then there was George Mueller, who raised some five millions from nothing. And Vashni Young, who afterwards wrote *"A Fortune to Share,"* could tell you of dozens who were hopelessly in debt, some who were sick, some sunk in despair, yet by contacting this Law, very one won through, some to fame, fortune and honors, all to contentment and happiness.

Mind you, it was not from us that this knowledge came to them But they did learn the working of the law, and out of that knowledge came good to them.

For ten years now, Robert Collier has been studying this law and how it works. For ten years he has been writing a course of 24 Lessons showing clearly and unmistakably how to use the Law to win success. And a couple of years ago, he made ready to publish this Course.

His first pre-publication price was $28.00, but people wrote asking why he could not put it up in less expensive form and sell it at a figure within easy reach of all. So he took the most important essentials from all the 24 lessons, re-wrote them in short, readable form, put them into seven brief, meaty Lessons and called them *"The God in You."*

To those who will mail the enclosed Coupon right away, I am going to send these seven Lessons, NOT at $28.00, BUT FOR LESS THAN A FIFTH OF THAT *PRICE—only* $4.85!

Mind you, these seven Lessons contain all the ESSENTIALS, the real meat, of the originally planned 24 Lesson Course. There is not as much explanation, and no unnecessary detail, but everything USABLE is there in a form you can readily understand and put into immediate practice.

Will you TRY these seven meaty lessons, if I send them to you subject to 30 days' examination, to be returned and your $4.85 refunded in full if you are not more than satisfied! Will you read them, put them to the test, watch them work in your life and your career?

Remember, you not only have 30 days in which to examine and try them before we regard it as a sale, but even after the 30 days are up, you get this additional guarantee.

If within six months your $4.85 has not brought you at least $300 of ADDITIONAL EARNINGS, send back the Lessons and I'll refund to you cheerfully and in full *every cent you have paid to me for them!*

There are no conditions and no strings of any kind to this offer. If within six months these Lessons have not shown you how to use the Law of Increase to bring you what you want, then they are not for you. Send them back and you get your money!

So don't decide about buying now. You can do that later. Send me now only the Coupon enclosed, with your name and address on it. Then, AFTER the 30 days are up, AFTER you have put the Law of

Increase to the test, you can decide whether or not you want to keep the Lessons. If you decide to return them, I'll pay the charges both ways.

But it is important that you send the Coupon right away, for I printed a special Gift Edition last Winter, very attractively done, and I have only a few of these left. If your order comes while we still have copies of this Gift Edition, I will have one personally inscribed to you and AUTOGRAPHED by the Author.

So if you want to try out your hidden powers without cost and without obligation, mail the enclosed Coupon NOW, while it is in your hand, before anything comes along to make you forget it.

Yours for DREAMS COME TRUE,

INCOME BUILDERS

* * *

If you are interested, I'll be glad to send you other letters that were used in following up these inquiries. All were profitable. All were mailed third class, under $0.01 cent postage, and together they brought the response up to about 30%.

This is good, but not unusually high for advertising inquiries. Robinson's Course sold for $28.00, payable $1.00 with order, $2.25 a month, and I understand that he sells something like 25% of those who respond to his ads. There is money in that, as you can judge from the fact that every year from 1930 on he did a business in excess of $150,000 year, and last year I believe the figure was over $500,000.

Almost any sort of course lends itself to this form of advertising.

Suppose you know a method of selling that has proven unusually successful for one salesman and that you believe all would be salesmen could use to advantage. Take the classified columns of the newspapers suggested above, or the columns of such magazines as *Opportunity, How to Sell, Pathfinder* or *Popular Mechanics*, all of which are good mail order pullers, and put in some such ad as the following:

* * *

This Man's True Story

Gives you the secret of how to make your fortune as a salesman. He has helped scores of inexperienced men and women to reach the highest rungs of the ladder of success as salesmen. He guarantees that he can help you, if you will let him. No cost and no obligation. Just your name and address on a postcard will bring you full particulars by mail.

* * *

To those who answer you might send first a short letter, handwritten if you wished, though the type-written or printed is easier to do. However, a personal hand-written message always gets the most attention. Here is the sort of copy that pulls. Bring in some personal experience where you can, and mention definite names and places. They help to carry conviction. And as a seeming afterthought, put in a postscript giving a strong testimonial.

* * *

Here is a True Story that Gives You

The Secret of How to Make a Fortune as a Salesman!

Dear Reader,

When I turned to selling as a last desperate chance to get out of debt, I was past middle age. I had no business experience whatever. I had a wife and young children to support, and I had no money. Worse still, I was hopelessly in debt.

My only capital was the knowledge of certain theoretical principles that I had worked out during years of study.

So fully did I believe in them, so strongly convinced was I that they would make a successful salesman of any man, that I took a job as a salesman on commission, pushing doorbells.

From the very first week, I was successful. For years, my sales topped those of every man in a great sales organization. I made a small fortune, just from "bell-pushing."

Then I made a second fortune training other men in the methods that had made me so successful.

Many men and women have paid me $10 each to learn these methods. Now I have put them in Course form so any man can learn them at small cost.

SEND NO MONEY! Just return the enclosed order

form and I will mail you the 7-Lesson Course that tells you the simple formula that turned an inexperienced, middle-aged man into a star salesman, and that has shown many other people how to turn failure into success.

Sincerely,

P. S. Here is what So-and-so says of this Course: (Quote). What it did for him and scores of others, it should do for you, too. But you run no risk. If it should not come up to your expectations in every way, you have only to return it within 30 days, and your money goes back to you in full at once.

RESERVATION No. 17

Please Return This Reservation at Once!

Subject to 30 days' Trial, you may send to me the seven Lessons on the New Kind of Salesmanship. When the Postman delivers them, I will deposit with him the sum of $2.98, plus the small postage charges. On this distinct understanding: If for any reason I return the Lessons within 30 days, you are to refund my $2.98 immediately.

Name

Address

City   State

*We pay postage when $2.98 is sent with order.

* * *

Ten days or two weeks later, follow up those who have not answered with some such letter as this.

* * *

With This Letter I Am Sending You
"How John Jones Won the Sales Contest!"

Dear Customer:

John Jones' name is fictitious—but his experience is typical of scores who have learned this secret of selling and amazed themselves and all their associates at the result. It will set you thinking, because what John Jones did, YOU can do. He is a good example of the scores of men and women that I have taught to SELL, and not only sell, but to grow into bigger, more successful, RICHER people in every way.

You see, I was not one of these "born salesmen," men who are endowed by Nature with such abundant energy and vitality and hail-fellow-well-met good-fellowship that they can go up to any stranger and by their sheer affability make friends with him in a few minutes.

On the contrary, I am retiring in disposition, never the kind to thrust myself forward. I was the typical "introvert," immersed in my own thoughts, absent-minded, quiet and unassuming, the last man on earth anyone would have picked for a successful "door-bell-pusher."

Yet from my very first week as a salesman, I earned $100 to $200 a week in COMMISSIONS!

How did I do it?

To begin with, I took the "canned" sales talk that the Sales Manager sent me and threw it in the waste-basket. Then I put into practice the principles of selling that I had worked out in theory from years of study. I took all my theoretical knowledge of human nature, all I had learned of psychology, and with it I perfected a sales approach that was unbeatable.

For years, I was the leader in a selling field where only experts survived. Then, a small fortune in my pockets, I took to teaching others the secret of my success. Many men and women cheerfully paid $10.00 to learn that secret. Hundreds of others have bought my course, have paid good money to learn my secret.

Now I have put all my experience, all my personal knowledge of selling and knack of training others to sell, into a course of seven lessons. And of this course, I can say— "I have helped many others to win success. I guarantee that I can help you, too." Hundreds of sets of this course have already been sold. Of the original edition, we have on hand 200 copies. A new edition is in the making, which when ready, is to sell for $5.00. While these few copies of the old edition last, you can get one for $2.98. You need, SEND NO MONEY!

Just your name on the enclosed Order Form will bring you a set of these seven lessons on *"The New*

Kind of Salesmanship" in the original edition, subject to 30 days' trial. If they don't show you the Secret of Selling, if they don't open for you the door to riches and success, send them back, and get your money. There are no strings to that offer. Your money is yours when you ask for it. Return the lessons and your $2.98 goes back to you at once.

But, remember, we have only 200 copies to sell at the $2.98 price. When they are gone, only the new edition will be available, and that will cost you $5.00. So if you want a glimpse of these amazing Lessons at the special low price, send your Reservation NOW!

Sincerely,

* * *

A folder telling "How John Jones won the sales contest" should accompany the letter. This can be a personal experience story, preferably with the picture of the man who writes it, telling how your Course enabled him to come up from the bottom and win out over scores experienced men.

Two weeks later, send out the same letter, with a memorandum attached to the top of it, with a penned note on it in ink to this effect:

* * *

Dear Mr. Jones:

Since I wrote you a couple of weeks ago, more than a hundred people have asked me to send them copies of my new method of selling. John Smith of this city just telephoned me that it had already been worth more than $300 in commissions to him.

But I haven't heard from YOU. So I am sending you a copy of my last letter, and I am holding out one copy of the Course for you.

Won't you let me hear from you . . . soon?

Sincerely,

***

A blue slip, with such a message on it, attached to a letter, frequently brings even better returns than did the original letter. It makes a most effective follow-up.

Half a dozen variations of the original appeal can also be used follow-ups. One of the most effective ways of using them is to have a letter on the letterhead of some former subscriber directed to your prospect and telling him how the course brought so much of good to this subscriber that he wants to see others profit from it as he has, and therefore he is taking the liberty of urging the prospect to send for the course.

Most advertising inquiries need half a dozen follow-ups to exhaust their sales possibilities. Many people claim to sell half of all their advertising inquiries. A few say they sell 70% of them. Almost any-should be able to sell 25%, because few people will answer unless they are truly interested and are seriously considering buying.

Here is a schedule outlining the method of handling inquiries and way to mail your follow-ups:

1. Make a card for each inquiry, showing name, address, key number of advertisement, and data received.

2. Address a correspondence envelope, stamping it in lower left hand corner— "This is the booklet you sent for." Enclose Letter No. 1, with booklet or other item offered in your advertisement, testimonial and order form and return envelope, and mail third class, using two ½ cents stamps, pre-cancelled. Key order form and booklet with a date stamp representing the week in which the inquiry is received. All inquiries received from Monday to Saturday bear the date of that Monday.

   Remember that 200 or more letters must be mailed at one time to Use 1 cent Postage, and that the letters must be sorted by states and cities. Otherwise they require 1 ½ cents Postage.

3. File the file card geographically by state, town and city, and the alphabetically by name under each city, in that particular week's file. Keep each week's card separately, with a master file card covering each weekly lot, on which master card must be entered the date the first follow-up letter is mailed and the date of all succeeding mailings.

4. Two weeks after mailing the first follow-up letter, address a monarch envelope to every card in that week's file. Then fill in at the top of Letter No. 2 the date and the salutation "Dear Mr. Jones." Key order blank and booklet with the date that this lot of inquiries was received, and with the additional numeral "2" to signify second follow-up to them. Enclose letter, booklet, order blank and return envelope, and mail out third class, using 2 cents stamps. Note on Master File Card the date and number of the follow-up

5. Two weeks later, send Follow-up No. 3. This will consist of original letter, with the memo slip attached to it; all enclosures will be the same. Key order blank and booklet with the date the inquiries were received adding the number

"3" to signify that this is the third follow-up. Enter on the Master File Card the fact that Follow-up No. 3 has been sent, the date of mailing and the number mailed.

6. Two weeks later, send Follow-up Letter No. 4, handling in the same way as for No. 3, but Using Key 4 added to the date.

7. Two weeks later, send Follow-up No. 5, adding "5" to the date on the order blank and booklet.

8. Two weeks later, send Follow-up No. 6 adding "6" to the date on order blank and booklet.

As orders are received from these mailings, the names, addresses and key numbers will indicate from what group they came, so they will get no more follow-ups and the cards for these should be pulled from the files. All Original inquiries can be destroyed after cards have been made for them.

Every kind of self-help book or course lends itself to this form of advertising, as do many kinds of merchandise It is one of the easiest ways to start a mail order business on little money, because all it needs is a dollar or two for the Classified Ad.

When the inquiries come in, if they are local, you can call upon them personally and sell your book or your service if you have not the money to have letters printed. Or you can pen your own letters and probably get a better response than you would if you had them printed

The great thing is to put your heart into them. It is always well, then possible, to call on a few of your inquiries, just to learn the kind of people you are writing to, what it is they want, what is most likely to interest them. Then carry the picture of these people in your mind then you write other inquirers. Make your letter personal. Make it sincere. Build on the solid foundation of honest service and you can then go back to these same customers and sell them anything else you may have.

That's all very well for you who know the business, perhaps you are thinking, but how am I to find the right books or products to sell?

In Lesson II we gave you two of the best offers of this kind that we know of. You will find others in the remaining lessons, and from time to time we expect to write you telling of new opportunities as we hear of them.

Meantime, if you want a Course on Salesmanship, there is a good and unusual one published by the Selavision Company of Greensboro, North Carolina. You will have no difficulty, I believe, in getting from them a generous wholesale price even on small test quantities.

If you'd like to try out *"The God in You"* Course, we shall be glad to furnish you copies of the *"God Never Ordered It Thus"* booklets at a price of $1.00 a hundred booklets. These booklets carry our name and address, but you could easily stamp your own over it, or paste sticker on it giving your name and address.

Copies of *"The God In You"* to fill resultant orders retail at $4.85. We shall be glad to furnish these to you at a price of $2.50 each. You could then follow up these buyers with other books and courses.

There will be plenty of things to sell, and at goodly margins of profit. All you have to do is to build your customer list.

LESSON IV

HOW TO MOVE YOUR PROSPECTS TO ACTION

Ten years ago there was a young man in a small Connecticut town with a book and an idea. The book was written for serious-minded men, to help show them the way to success. He had an idea that he ought to be able to sell it to every ambitious man and woman. But that required money. And he had only a couple of hundred dollars to his name.

What Would You Do With $200?

This young man didn't lack for courage. He was entirely willing to stake his all on his judgment. The question was, how to do it? As an appropriation for a publicity campaign, $200 was a joke. Bookstores? Posters? Circulars? *Mail order!* It would just pay for a page ad in one of the current events magazines that was largely read by the better type of serious-minded men.

He took his problem to this magazine and got their help in laying out his ad. Being book-sellers themselves, they knew the kind of copy that would most appeal to the book-buyer. And they helped him to put that kind of copy into his ad. Today, any good Advertising Agency that has had mail order experience would be glad to write the entire ad for him, without cost to him.

The magazine came out. Nothing happened. Two or three days passed. Still not an order. He'd about decided to bid that $200 "Good-bye!" Then a single order came straggling in. He welcomed it like a long-lost brother. Next day three or four. Then they started coming in bunches.

From that first ad, costing his $200, he got $2,000 worth of orders for his book.

$200 Grown Into Thousands

That $200 was the start of a fortune. With the $2,000 he got from his orders, he immediately placed more ads, and as the orders kept rolling in, branched out into other magazines. In the years that have elapsed since then, that young man has sold $2,000,000 worth of books. *All by mail!*

That young man was A. L. Pelton of Meriden, Connecticut. The book, *"Power of Will."* And the magazine that brought him such profitable results was the old *Review of Reviews*. Today that magazine is out of business, but there are numbers of others that bring just as profitable returns as ever the *Review* did in its heyday, and even better results can be received from the same money put into circulars.

Thirty years ago selling books by mail was in its infancy. A few encyclopedias, a history or two, perhaps a dozen other serious works were being marketed by mail in a small way. But the field was practically virgin.

Today look at it! Every Encyclopedia, every History, every work of any consequence, is being advertised and sold by mail.

And think of the records some of them have made! $2,000,000 worth of a single Encyclopedia sold in a year, $1,000,000 worth of O. Henry's short stories sold by mail in a year—and the same thing repeated the following year! Over a hundred different publishers selling books by mail, some of them in vast quantities. The *Review of Reviews* alone averaged more than $1,000,000 worth a year for a number of years. Yet every one of them started small, frequently with only a few hundred dollars.

What Every Publisher Knows

Why is it that some books sell only in the hundreds, where others, subtle or no better written, little or no more interesting into the hundred thousands?

Books are made to sell, and the real profits in book publishing begin just where most publishers leave off, after the first or second thousand.

The reason some books sell in such vast quantities and others have difficulty in closing out a first edition is frequently a matter only of the kind of selling that is put behind them.

Take the well-known books on Etiquette as an instance. Who would have thought, a few years ago, that a set of books on Etiquette, of all subjects, could be successfully marketed in the hundred thousands.

Yet considerably over a million such books were sold in a couple years!

And the joke of it was that one of the most successful of these books had been lying on the publishers' shelves for ten years, just as it was lying on the shelves in the bookstores - gathering dust, selling perhaps a few score copies in the course of the year—waiting for the man to come along and present its possibilities to the public in a new way.

What started its sale? Not money . . ., but a new idea . . ., the "What's Wrong With This Picture?" idea. It made people etiquette conscious, fearful that they might be committing gaucheries, making ourselves laughing-stocks. So they bought the Book of Etiquette to learn how they should conduct themselves under given sets of circumstances. And the sale still goes on.

It didn't take much money to start that sale. As with Pelton's *"Power of Will,"* a single ad costing $200 showed the publishers that they had the right idea. A thousand circulars costing less than $50 confirmed the results of the ad. After that, it was merely a matter of multiplication . . . , reaching more people, making bigger profits.

Making an Unknown Author

Take O. Henry. How many people had heard of him before the *Review* took hold of his works? And today his name is a household word. More of his short stories have been sold than of any writer, living or dead.

Yet there are doubtless hundreds of authors whose stories would have as great an appeal to just as many people, if only they were presented to them in as interesting a way. It was advertising that sold them by the million a year. It was advertising; advertising of the "different" sort, but keyed-coupon advertising and circularizing, that brought in as high as $100,000 worth of mail orders from a single ad in one medium.

Robert Louis Stevenson is one of the "Immortals," but would his works ever have been sold in quantity to the "masses" without the same sort of interesting advertising? Even Kipling, great as he was, would never have had the vogue he has if the advertising of his stories had not been as unique in its way as are the stories themselves.

Harold Bell Wright, Gene Strattan Porter, Zane Gray; what was it gave them their popularity, their enormous sales? Advertising. Clever, arresting, advertising; interesting. eye-catching as the stories themselves

Fields Yet Untouched

There are so many phases of life and activity—so many different facets to our everyday round—that twenty years from now publishers will be saying (as we said about twenty years ago) that in our day the field was practically virgin.

The enormous sales of the etiquette books, of Wells' *"Outline of History,"* of O. Henry, of the Eliot Five Foot Shelf, of Dale Carnegie's *"How to Make Friends and Influence People,"* show what can be done.

It's merely a matter of finding the primal human motive that a book appeals to, be it love or gain or fear or caution, and then directing all your advertising at that one motive.

And the fact that it has been tried before or even done before doesn't preclude your doing it, provided you can do it in a way new and different. After the pioneer in the Etiquette field had sold over 300,000 sets, other publishers sold as many more of competing books, even while he was again doubling his sales on the original book.

The fact of the matter is that the field is so vast that the interest one creates stimulates the sales of all.

Starting at the Very Beginning

What is the first thing to do if planning a mail order book ad or circular?

Before you put pen to paper, before you ring for your stenographer, decide in your own mind what effect you want that ad to produce on your reader; what motive it must appeal to; what feeling it must create in him to make him want your book more than the money it will cost him.

Only the new ad-writer selects the arguments that are nearest at hand; the viewpoints that appeal to him. The important thing is to be able to put yourself in the other fellow's shoes and discuss things that interest him rather than the things that interest you.

Read your book yourself. See what you get from it. Are you richer, more cultured or more efficient for having read it? Does it help your standing with other people? Does it show you how to do anything, write anything, and say anything better than you could before? Is something every man should know? Does it gratify any passion? Does it show you how to help those you love? Does it prevent mistakes that might cost you money, or the respect of others?

The Motive's the Thing

Ask yourself a few such questions as these. Then pick the motive that is strongest and present it from the point of view of your reader. Show him what it will do for him, what it will get him, what he wants most that it will give him. Descriptions of your book, no matter how interesting, will never sell it by the hundred thousands. It's *what it will do* for the man who buys it that counts.

It can be done, with every book, which has any reason for being. Books that are apparently sold out can be revived with new appeals and sold bigger than ever before. Books that are just out can be sold the scores of thousands instead of single editions. Many a business been started on "Publishers' Remainders" and damaged sets.

It was the new appeal in its advertising that put the Five Foot Shelf over when it was ready to be dropped. It was a new appeal that made Wells' *"Outline of History"* sell in its third year bigger even than its first and second.

Flagging the Reader's Attention

Your reader, looking over the pages of a magazine, gets a series of impressions just as you might if you were looking from the window of a moving train. You catch a fleeting glimpse of some object. You turn for a closer inspection. If that interests you, you observe every detail carefully—otherwise your glance wanders off again in search of some more interesting object.

There are hundreds of other ads in every magazine, competing with yours for attention. Unless yours has something about it that stands out from the mass—that catches his eye—that arouses his interest—on he goes to the next one.

Your first problem is to find some point of contact, some feature that will flag your reader's interest, which will make your ad stand out from all the others the moment he glances at the first line of it.

The One Thing You Are Most Interested In Is <u>You</u>

Every man is constantly holding a mental conversation with himself, and the burden of that conversation is himself; his interests, his loved ones his business, his advancement.

The surest way to flag his interest is to chime in on that conversation with a thought along those same lines.

*"Are you satisfied
just to keep the wolf from the door?"*

"The odds are 94 to 6 against you!"

*"What to do—the question that makes men
or breaks them."*

"How much do you know?"

*"Which of these men has learned
the secret of 15 minutes a day"*

*"How Mrs. Brownell became
the most popular hostess in town...."*

Headlines such as these will fit right in with the thoughts of any man or woman; will flag their interest; will make them read on.

They are the most successful kind of interest-flagger, but many
books do not lend themselves to such headlines. That is when the
ad-writer's real ingenuity must come into play. For out of every
book you can get some startling headline. It may come from the
book itself. It may be something about it that ties up with the news
of the day. It may make news itself.

News! News! News!

What the world wants, and has wanted since the beginning, is news.
The business world is no exception. If you can tell a man something
new, you can get his attention. Give it a personal twist, or show its
relation to his business, and you have his interest.

Do you know how Wells' *"Outline of History"* was first put across?
On its news value!

"The Oldest Man in the World."

"Was this the Flood of the Biblical Story!"

"The Finding of Moses."

Newspaper headlines, all of them! News interest in every one of
them. Rich man, poor man, beggar man, thief. All stop to read if
you can put news interest into your headline.

"When the Rattlesnake Struck!" Can't you see yourself reading on to
see what happens? Well, that was what thousands of others did
every time that ad was run. It was the most successful O. Henry ad
ever written.

"What is the Unpardonable Sin in all Nature?" Can you imagine any
reader so blasé as not to go on at least a few lines farther to find the
answer to that question? And if you can lead him on these few lines,
it's your own fault if you can't make your story sufficiently

interesting to carry him on down to your coupon and its dotted line.

The Part the Picture Plays

Should every book ad have a picture? Should you show the book?

There is no doubt that an attractive, appropriate illustration helps the pulling power of any ad. But the picture must be part of the story. It's an attention-getter primarily, and it must get the right kind of attention. The picture of a pretty girl, done in sufficiently startling manner, will always get attention; but it may not be the kind that will impel anyone to read your ad. The picture must lead them right into your story to be of any value to you. It must tie up with your headline, with the story itself.

A cut of your book is not essential, though it too helps. If you are advertising for inquiries, and offering a free or semi-free book, by all means show a picture of it. It has frequently increased returns by as much as 25%.

People like to see what they are getting, and next to having the article itself in front of them, is a good picture of it.

Getting Your Idea Across

After you have gotten your reader's attention, the next thing is to get your idea across, win his interest in your book itself, so describe it that he can see it as you see it.

A sale is made in a man's mind. Before you can get his order, it is necessary to register a sequence of impressions, the combined result of which will be to make him want the thing you are selling more than the money it costs.

After you have caught your reader's attention, after you have won his interest, there still remains this difficult job of getting your idea over, of picturing to him what your book has to offer.

The secret of success in it lies in picking first some feature he can easily grasp, some object or idea he is thoroughly familiar with, and then building on that. Here is the way one mail order company does it with fish:

* * *

"If you like mackerel that is white and juicy, thick-meated and fat, codfish that is tender and 'good-tasting,' lobster that's as sweet, fresh and dainty as though you had just taken it from the shell, let me supply you."

* * *

And another:

* * *

"Old age is merely our name for the gradual poisoning of our bodies. Aches and pains burrowing and creeping through the system, a relaxed abdomen, deepening lines on the face, jangling nerves, a haunting feeling of dullness and gloom, these outward signs indicate that actual poisons are being deposited in the blood, tissues and joints."

* * *

Do Your Building One Brick at a Time

The one thing to remember is this: Your reader can grasp but one idea at a time. As he reads your letter, he builds a picture with the words you give him like a child building a house with blocks. Give him, therefore, the basic, essential ones first, the little filling-in details later, else your whole structure will tumble down.

Start with the feature he can most readily comprehend—build upon that and make every additional feature advance the central idea; take him one step nearer the goal. If it won't do that, it is unnecessary and had better be cut.

In short, your problem is rather similar to that of the newspaper paragrapher. He sums up the meat of his story in two or three words in the headlines. Then he adds a sub-head, giving a few essential features. Then a few lines, elaborating or explaining these. With this framework to build upon, he fills in the details of his story.

Supplying the Reason Why

Most people are like cars. They can be pulled or pushed along, or they can be moved by starting up their own motive power from within. But in either case you've got to provide the fuel. And the fuel that will move your reader to the action you desire is arousing in him the right motive.

Exercising persuasion is simply a matter of showing your reader how taking the action you desire will benefit him—him or someone he loves. The benefit may not be a material one, it may be merely the fulfillment of a duty. But unless you have appealed in some way to one of the six primal human motives; Love, Gain, Duty, Pride, Self-indulgence, Self-Preservation; your ad lacks a reason for being, and your returns will show the lack.

There must be a definite scheme behind it, a reason for your offer, reason for the ad itself.

Summed up in words of two syllables, supplying the reason why insists of making your reader want your book, not by describing it but by showing him what it will do for *him,* how he will benefit by putting it into action, what he will lose by not having it.

Getting Action

Watch the crowd in front of a side show. At just the critical moment in the barker's talk, his assistants on the outside of the crowd start a general push forward toward the ticket window. Barnum long ago discovered the need of an impulse at the right moment to overcome our natural inertia.

The first thing to do is to find the motive your ad should arouse. Then you can look for some easy preliminary task on which that motive can be set to work. After that, it's merely a matter of making it easier for the reader, already started, to go forward than to go back.

You've got his interest. You've described your book, told him that it will do for him, and showed him his need of it. But he hasn't quite made up his mind. He balks at putting his name on the dotted line. "Some other time!" "Tomorrow!" That little word "Tomorrow!" lost more sales than all other causes put together.

So don't make him come to a definite decision right away. Let him put the decision off 'till the morrow, but get his action right away. "Send no Money!" or "Examine it for a week at our risk and expense!" or "Don't decide now. Let us send you _____ for a week, to read, to examine, to talk over with your family. Then decide!" or "You run no risk. Your money has a string to it. It isn't ours until you say so. You can have it back if you're willing to give back the book."

Get firmly fixed in your own mind just what you want him to, then make it so easy for him to do it that it is simpler to go ahead than to draw back.

The Clincher of the Ad

As the tail is to the kite, as the rudder to the ship, so is the close to the ad. It may be a perfectly good advertisement aside from that. It may fit right in with the reader's thoughts, it may win his interest, it may spur him to action, but if it doesn't tell him what to do, if it doesn't provide a penalty for his not doing it, your prospect will slip away from you like a fish off the hook.

There is just one reason *why* anyone ever reads an ad. He expects a reward. That is the key to holding his interest.

In the same way, there is only one reason why your reader will do as you want him to. He fears the penalty you hold over him. It may be the loss of money. It may be the fear of ridicule. It may be lack of advancement. But unless your close can inspire action through fear of loss of money or prestige or opportunity, it won't bring the results.

And to bring home that loss, be definite and be specific! If you are going to advance your price, say so! If possible, set a definite date for it! If the opportunity is limited, if you have only a few copies of a certain kind, if a particular binding is out of the ordinary, tell him so! Make your reader feel that this is his last chance. Keep that penalty for delay dangling before his mind's eye; the money, savings lost or the opportunity missed. Put into your close the fear of consequences.

What Do You Want the Reader to Do?

Finally, tell him *what* to do. We're all mentally lazy, so dictate his action for him. Get your suggester to working. If he is to do certain things, *describe* them. Tell him to "Put his name on the attached Coupon and drop in the mail." Or "Pin his check or a dollar bill to the bottom of this ad and mail."

Show him that he takes no chances in doing as you tell him. Quote the testimonials of prominent men. The testimony of other people, especially of those in positions of authority and those who would not be suspected of bias, has great convincing power. Submit the names of a few users. Or, best of all, give him a money-back-if-not-satisfied-guarantee.

But above all, tell your reader what it is you want him to do. Make it so plain and easy he won't have a reason on earth for not doing it. If you don't, you haven't finished your ad, and lacking the effect of that clincher, your reader is likely to lapse from his almost ready attitude back into indifference.

Taking the Risk Out of Publishing

Probably the greatest forward step in publishing in recent years is that your circulars or advertising can be made to take all the risks out of publishing.

How much does it cost you to print and bind an edition of 1,000 or 2,000 books! Would you be willing to spend a few dollars of this to find out in advance, beyond the question of a doubt, how well your book is going to sell? Whether it would pay you to make that edition 1,000, 5,000 or 25000? Or, whether you will save money by not publishing it at all?

A Delphian Oracle

That's where mail order advertising or circularizing can foretell the future. Write your ad. Word it just as you would if the book were already on the bookstore shelves. But make it a special "Advance of publication" offer. Give a reason for it. Offer an inducement for ordering then. Have the first few copies autographed by the author, or a specially numbered first edition. Then watch the results! If the ad well done, you'll get just as many orders from it as though the books were ready to deliver.

That's how Mail Order publishers work. You don't often hear of them being left with big lots of un-salable books on hand. To get the rights to their first edition of Wells' *History*, the *Review of Reviews* had to guarantee a sale of 83,000 sets in two years, and pay the royalty in advance!

But do you suppose they were taking any chance! Not at all. Before putting pen to that contract, before paying $1.00 of royalty, they tested out the pulling power of Wells, wrote a circular on it, sounded out its possibilities.

Then, when they agreed to sell 83,000 sets in two years, they were able to jump right in and sell 96,000 in little over three months. A year later, when they agreed to sell 100,000 of the four-volume sets in five years, they were able by the same process to dispose of all of them in fourteen months!

The Book of Gold did this same thing just a few years ago. Dr. Brown Landone had come to them with a new book about the Pyramid prophecies. He called it, *"Prophecies of Melchizedek, as Given in Great Pyramids and the Seven Temples."* He offered the sales rights to The Book of Gold. They agreed to publish the book, provided they could first test its selling possibilities.

So before they spent one cent to print the book, they wrote the following letter, and tested it in small quantities on a number of likely prospects.

* * *

This Letter Brings You a Message of Such Importance
That I Am Attaching Stamps for Your Reply!

Dear Customer:

This letter, coming to you in advance of any public announcement, is intended for your eyes alone. It contains information which we ask you to regard as confidential. You will see why in a moment.

So you may realize at the outset the peculiar importance of this message, let me tell you, before taking up the details, that I believe it brings you the answer to such questions as, "How long will this war last? Shall we be dragged into it? Will the 'Blitzkrieg,' when it comes, be successful, and if not, will a make-shift peace be made in the West, while Japan and Germany combine against Russia? When can we look for LASTING peace and real prosperity?"

Twenty years ago, the great leaders of the world assured us that the world was now safe for democracy and we would have a century of peace. Ten years later, business men and financiers prophesied another decade of amazing prosperity. A year and a half ago, the four leaders of Europe told us we should have peace for our generation. Today, our own government assures us that we shall never again be drawn into a world war.

As prophets and seers, the political and business leaders of the world have been woeful failures. They have been unable to foresee even a few months ahead.

In March of 1914, for instance, Brown Landone stated in public talks at the Sorbonne in Paris (and later in London) that a great European war would break out within six months. Officials everywhere ridiculed him. Yet *in five months all of Europe was at war.*

Three years ago in Minneapolis, before groups of 250 people, Landone foretold world events of vital importance for 1939, particularly on September 1st, 3rd, and 20th, November 25th and a number of other dates. On September 1st, Hitler marched into Poland. On the 3rd, Britain and France declared war. On the 20th, Poland was partitioned. On November 28th, Russia rejected Finland's final plea. A hundred years from now, that may be looked upon as one of the great important dates in world history, for on that day Russia changed from a passive to an active force for evil, taking the first step in what may well prove to be the downfall of Communism. And on every one of the later dates foretold by Landone, events of vital world importance took place.

Yet Brown Landone lays no claim to gifts of prophecy. He is a mathematician rather than a seer. He claims only to be able to READ the prophecies that were recorded in stone in the Temple of Temples 5,000 years ago, by men whose knowledge of future events seems to have been as far in advance of their age as was their understanding of mathematics and of the heavens.

It was not until the time of Pope Gregory that European civilization had a calendar of 365 days, with an allowance for leap year, yet 5,000 years ago, the builders of the Great Pyramid at Giza laid out each side of that Pyramid to the measurement of 365.2422 cubits. The exact number of days to the minute of the solar year!

We credit Copernicus and Galileo with discovering the movement of the heavenly bodies, yet those ancient builders of Temples and Pyramids appear to have known 5,000 years ago the exact time it takes for the universe to revolve around its center, and hundreds of other things that we fondly look upon as modern discoveries.

Not only that, but they conceived a unit of measurement far superior to anything we have today. All of our measures are uncertain. Our acre differs in different parts of the world. Our bushel is not the same as the bushel in England. Our tons are different. Even the measurement of the mile varies.

In contrast, those ancient Masters conceived a measurement of land based on the movement of the earth around the sun. Using 365.2422 as the circumference of a circle, they determined the area and then worked out a square of the same area and made it the unit of land measure. All other measurements were based on the length of one side of that square.

They knew man's past, and figured man's rate of progress so exactly that they seem to have been able to record in stone the exact dates of important events for thousands of years ahead. Their Teleois system of measurements, re-discovered by Dr. Landone, has been found of immeasurable help in unlocking knowledge of ages past, and in his opinion, it is the only certain guide ever found for revealing the time of future events.

Many books have been written about the prophecies of the Pyramid. They are said to have forecast to the day the beginning of the first World War, the date of the Armistice and many other events of world-wide importance. But many of the forecasts given since then have been wrong. And the reason is easy to see. In reading the numerical code left by the builders the writers of these books used only one-dimensional measurements—the linear distances from point to point. This was all right as long as they were in the passages leading up to the great Temple of Temples. But everything about the Temple of Temples itself is based on three-dimensional or cubical measurements, and must be read on that, basis. Not only that, but while the TIME of great events is determined by the cubic measurements, it is Landone's belief that the particular DAYS when these may be expected and the NATURE of the events is revealed only by the Teleois system of measurement.

"This Teleois system," says Dr. Landone, "is found in each of the seven great Temples of antiquity. It is the basis on which the whole universe is formed, for it is found in the proportions of the intervals of our musical scales, in the proportional distance of planets from the sun, in every bone in our bodies, even in the designs of snowflakes. It is the system of measurement that was used by the Wise Men of old to transmit their prophecies to us."

As Brown Landone reads these prophecies, (he has made a study of them for more than *25* years), they predict four World Wars, of which this is the third. Time first started in August, 1914. The second was an economic war, when one European nation brought the world ten years of depression by trying to dominate it through control of gold. The Third World War is now on. It will merge into the fourth, according to his reading of the Prophecy, and then we shall have PERMANENT peace.

Three times man has been given a prophetic vision of what lay ahead, and the chance to effect a transformation on earth. Three times man has been blind to that vision and to the help offered him. Today he is offered that vision of the future a fourth time. This time, we are told, man must attain his goal, or civilization will be submerged for 3,060 years.

In the Temple of Temples within the great Pyramid, according to Brown Landone, there is definite evidence that the builders recorded 1939 as time year when the world would enter the Great Transforming change. It was to begin August 10th, 1939, and end March 6th, 1947. After that, permanent peace…, *or chaos.*

What will happen between those two important dates? What can we do to help ourselves, individually, and as citizens of the world? Brown Landone believes that our path is marked out for us, our instructions clearly written so that all who will, may read; the dates symbolized in the Hall of Transforming Action are dates of what is now taking place, and what we can look to see happen over the next eight years. He believes that this prophetic wisdom, if used as a guide, will enable us to make our lives secure and happy, to reach heights never before attained by man.

"For twenty-five years I have been using these prophetic charts for my own certain guide," says Landone, "and never yet have they failed me." Now he is nearing the century mark (his youngest grandchild is 34), and it is his ambition to leave behind him a work that will help mankind on its way. So he has put into manuscript form *"The Prophecy of Melchizedek,"* as recorded in stone in the Temple of Temples within the Great Pyramid, and now revealed by means of the re-discovered system of Teleois in measurements.

That manuscript has not yet been printed and may *never be printed.* Whether it will be or not, depends partly upon you. I am writing you today to find out if you and enough others like you are interested in hearing what lies ahead, whether you really want to do something' to help bring about peace and, security or whether this Prophecy will be treated as indifferently as were the three great Prophecies of olden days, and might therefore be just as well left untold.

The answer to that question is so important that I am enclosing stamps for use in sending your reply. But because the answer may be "No," I am asking you to say nothing about this letter until it has been decided whether or not the Prophecy shall be printed.

Will you tell me what you think on the enclosed card?

SEND NO MONEY! Just say on the enclosed card whether, *if the Prophecy is printed,* you will be interested enough to pay the low Pre-publication price of $1.00 for it to the Postman when he delivers it, on the distinct understanding that you can return it within 30 days and get your $1.00 back at once.

That low Pre-publication price of $1.00 is no indication of the value of this great Prophecy. Even from the ordinary book-making point of view, the material that enters into it should bring much more than that. But $1.00 is a high enough price to tell us whether or not you are interested, Would you risk $1.00 to find out what's ahead in 1940? Would that be too much to pay for a reliable guide in the uncertain days to come?

Sincerely,

P.S. If you care to send your $1.00 now, we will return it within 10 days if it is decided not to publish the Prophecy. If we do publish it, you will get one of the first copies off the press, POSTPAID, and with it, with our compliments, a FREE copy of Robert Collier's latest little book, *"The Kingdom of Expansion."*

Please Return This Card At Once!

Special Pre-Publication Offer No. 37

The Book of Gold
152 West 42nd Street
New York, N. Y.

YES—I should be interested in seeing *"The Prophecy of Melchizedek,"* as recorded in stone in the Temple of Temples of the Great Pyramid.

If it is published within the next 30 days, you may send a copy to me. When the Postman delivers it, I will pay him $1.00, plus the small postage charges.* (We pay all charges, if you send your $1.00 with this card.)

On this understanding: I can return the *Prophecy* at any time within 30 days after I receive it, and you are to refund my $1.00 at once.
Name

Address

City   State

*If you care to send your $1.00 with this card now, we will pay the postage, *and in addition,* we will send you Robert Collier's latest little book, *"The Kingdom of Expansion"*—FREE! You get your $1.00 back just the same if you return *"The Prophecy of Melchizedek"*, or if it is not published at once.

* * *

From that letter, they got such good results that they immediately ordered 25,000 copies of the book and prepared to mail 250,000 circular letters. Within six months, they sold 45,000 copies of the *"Prophecies of Melchizedek."*

The big profits from that sale came . . . NOT from *"The Prophecies of Melchizedek"*, but from the sale of additional books to the people who bought that one. Landone had other books, and these were immediately offered, and sold in huge volume. The Book of Gold had other books, too, and these sold in highly profitable volume. Even if no profit had been made on the Prophecy book, the mailing would have been a big success because of the fine new customer list it built, and the number of additional books sold to them.

Don't Wait Until You Bury an Author

You don't have to wait until an author is dead and buried before advertising his works. You don't even have to wait until he has written more than one book.

If you are "sold" on an author, you can develop him as a future asset just as much as the *Review of Reviews* developed O. Henry. You can sell his first book or books—and at the same time be building an audience for all his future works.

You know that the best prospect for an author's later books is the man who has read one or more of his earlier ones. What would it be worth to you to have in your files the names of each of your author's former buyers? What would it be worth to you in sales if, the moment you brought out a new book, you could send a full description and order card to every purchaser of previous books by that same author? How big would your editions run—how high your profits?

Yet that is exactly what mail order advertising enables you to do. That is one of the secrets of the enormous sales of the subscription book houses. They have accumulated vast lists of book-buyers, and they sell to them over and over again.

To Sum Up

The ad of your book must contain these six essential elements:

1st—The Headline and Opening, which fits into the reader's thoughts and establishes a 'point of contact with his interests, thus arousing his curiosity and prompting him to read further.

2nd— The Description, which pictures your book to him by first outlining its essential features and then filling in the necessary details.

3rd—The Reason Why, which creates in your reader's mind a desire for your book by describing—not the book itself—but what it will do for him, the riches, the pleasure, the benefit he will derive from it.

4th—The Proof, which offers to the reader proof of the truth of your statements, or establishes confidence by a money-back-if-not-satisfied guarantee.

5th—The Penalty, which gets immediate action by holding over your reader's head the loss in money, or prestige, or opportunity that will be his if he does not act at once.

6th—The Close, which tells the reader just what to do and how to do it, and makes it easy for him to act at once.

As to How Long Your Ad Should Be

Some authorities will tell you to write only short, crisp ads, with plenty of white space—others to crowd in every word you can get. Both are wrong. There is no hard and fast rule as to how long an ad should be, except that it should be long enough to tell your story, but short enough to hold your reader's interest.

As a general proposition, an ad in which you are seeking only inquiries should be short, merely leading the reader down to the free booklet and the coupon. Whereas an ad in which you are attempting to make the actual sale should be long enough to tell all about your offer.

Lincoln covered it pretty well when someone asked him how long a man's legs should be, "They should be long enough to reach the ground."

Let us take a couple of test cases and see exactly how a first book by an unknown author and a new publisher can be sold. The copy that follows was written for a woman whom the public had never heard of, using her own name as the publisher of her own book.

It was not even an advertisement. It was printed in small type on both sides of a postcard, and mailed to lists of people who had bought books on psychology or self-improvement from other publishers. Such lists can easily be had from any good list broker such as W. Maddern of 215 Fourth Avenue, New York, New York and Mosley Selective List Bureau of 38 Newbury Street, Boston, Massachusetts.

The copy follows.

* * *

I Have Discovered a Secret That Startles Me

But It Has Proven to Be an Aladdin's
Lamp. It Gives Me Anything I want.

You must have had that strange feeling (almost everyone does) that you have done the thing you are doing at the moment, before. Suddenly, you say to yourself, "Why! I have lived here before, in some previous life. I walked on this beach a million years ago. This pretty house that I have just moved into . . ., I am *moving back* into this house. This is where I used to live, ages ago!"

It comes to everyone, this peculiar impression of having been through exactly the same experience before. With some it comes often, and is very distinct, the actual words that others and yourself are speaking being clearly remembered; or the exact appearance of a room, its dimensions, decorations, furniture, coloring, odor being precisely as it seemed to you on a previous occasion With others, the experience is more vague and less frequent. Yet it happens to everyone the mysterious thing about it being that you know, as an actual physical fact, that you never really did, in the flesh of your present incarnation, actually have that experience before.

The Key to Happiness

I am not a psychologist amateur or professional. I am an average American business worker, with an average education as a background and have given no more thought to metaphysics mental sciences and religions than one runs across in the ordinary course of casual reading and human experience. Yet this strange phenomenon of "having been there before" has occurred to me so frequently of late that I set about solving it, with the determination with which one would attack a knotty business problem

"Perhaps," said I to a friend who is a practitioner of a well known mental science, "I have stumbled across a new idea in metaphysics."

My friend smiled. Said he, "You have revealed to yourself the last, ultimate secret of every religion, every system of metaphysics and mental science on the face of the earth. You have the secret, the KEY to happiness health, wealth and the things you desire. If everybody knew what you know, there would be no need for religions or systems or codes; no need for books, or lectures, or courses. All new thought sciences are based on a central idea so simple, that it can he expressed in one sentence. The difficulty that confronts teachers is in making their religion, or system, or science difficult!

"Experience proves that there must be a lot of preliminary talk, or study, or reading. If this is not given, the student would feel he had not gotten his money's worth. . . or, having come upon your secret so easily, would have too little respect for it."

Nothing You Desire That You Cannot Have

This startled me, you may be sure. I spent some time wording my precious secret into plain language, and went to some trouble to look up leaders of a dozen other metaphysical systems and religions. Each one, in turn, on reading my paper, reacted in much the same manner. "Certainly," each said, in effect, "that is the secret of happiness on earth. Put that to work in your daily life (and it is easy) and there is nothing on this earth that you desire, that you cannot have!"

Well, this amazing secret has done wonders for me and all the friends I have told about it. It is actually like an Aladdin's lamp. I merely have to desire a new car, or a trip to Europe, or relief from pain, or a solution of business, domestic or household problems and behold, I have it! My secret is not a new religion, or a new system of mental science. It is the spark, the enlivening spirit of every religion. Every follower of every system of thought will immediately realize the full benefit, the complete promise of his religion, if he uses this secret, amazing revelation that I discovered quite by accident. My secret clarifies, beautifies, strengthens and endears the chosen religion or science to the student.

Worth $1,000 in a Year's Time

I have no desire to make money out of my discovery. I don't need money. My secret gives me all I can use. I have no more right to make a profit on revealing my discovery to others than the Mayor has to charge for a city's air. Yet it does cost something to tell my story and something more to have the secret printed and mailed to those who would like to examine it.

It is worth everything to you, as it has been to me and my friends. In actual money, it could be worth at least a thousand dollars to you, in a year's time or less. Yet, as I say, it is yours as much as the air is yours. But, distribution costs require me to ask a dollar for my newly discovered secret, which ought to just about pay for these costs. I call it the "So-and-So Secret." The secret is in the first sentence—then I use about 3,500 words to make it entirely clear to you, with many practical examples of the secret's application.

Five Days' Trial

I want you to send for "So-and-So Secret" and read it through (it will take 10 minutes each time) every day for 5 days. If you don't think the "So-and-So Secret" is going to do for you what it did for me—just return it and I will return the dollar. Fill in the blanks below and send this card with remittance to my publishers today!

Name

Address

City,   State

Send me the "So-and-So Secret" described above, for which I enclose one dollar. I understand that I may have my dollar back if not satisfied.

Name

Address

City   State

Mail this card with $1.00 to address above.

* * *

That card brought back more than 5,000 orders, each accompanied by $1.00 payment. It was a highly profitable mailing.

When immediate cash is not such a great consideration, and it seems more important to build a big list of interested customers, it is a good plan to offer your book ON APPROVAL subject to a week's free examination. You usually get from 3 to 5 times as many orders from a FREE EXAMINATION offer as from one for cash, and as a rule, the returns and losses seldom run to 25%, so you end up with considerably more business. Here is an example of a postcard mailing on the FREE EXAMINATION basis:

* * *

Will You Look at a Copy of
"HOW TO GET WHAT YOU WANT"
If I Send It To You FREE?

In days of old, alongside the road leading to a certain city, there was said to dwell a Sphinx. To every traveler who wished to enter the city the Sphinx propounded a riddle which, if he failed to answer, he was devoured.

That was the famous Riddle of the Sphinx of olden times. But today there is one just as difficult—and those who fail to answer it are just as surely devoured by poverty and want. It is, *"How can I earn more money?"*

It was to answer this riddle that the two volumes of *"How to Get What You Want"* were written. And that they do answer it is attested by the scores of letters we receive every day like this one from Savannah, Georgia.

"They have been a turning point in my life. I am today a far better man morally, physically and especially financially. From a financial point of view, I am $1500 better off and on the road to make real money."

—H. P. H.

Will you examine these two volumes if I send them to you FREE? Examine them for a week, read them and TRY them out! No money, no risk and no obligation.

Just make sure that your name and address as given on the other side of this card are correct, and mail it back to us. By return Parcel Post —prepaid— the two volumes of *"How to Get What You Want"* will come to you for a week's FREE EXAMINATION and TRIAL.

———————

YES! I will examine the two volumes of *"HOW TO GET WHAT YOU WANT"* if you send them to me FREE!

You may send me postpaid for a week's FREE EXAMINATION, the two volumes of "How to Get What You Want."

I will either return them at the end of the week, or send you $1.98 in full payment.

Name

If you remit your $1.98 with this order, we will send you—FREE—a   copy   of   *"ACRES   OF*

DIAMONDS," the book that made more than
$4,000,000.

* * *

Any idea you may develop for money-saving, for self-improvement,
lends itself to such an offer. You may have a new method for
bettering your position. I know a man who worked out such an idea
and sold 11,000 of them at $12.50 each in about six months' time.

You may have a new method of beauty culture, of exercise, of
treating or relieving some ailment. You may know how to prevent
baldness, how to relieve rupture, how to cure athlete's foot.
Whatever you have, here is a way you can easily present it to your
logical prospects, lists of whom you can always get through list
brokers like those mentioned before.

Just as an example of how such ideas may be presented, I given
below a letter written by a Brooklyn Publisher on a new and
unknown book he was bringing out, a book that the letter sold in
big quantities.

* * *

Dear Reader:

Will you let me send you for seven days'
examination a copy of a startling little book which
conceivably may inspire you to make more money
during 1947 than you have for the past five years?

This book has had an amazing effect on the men
and women who have read it.

For instance, the ideas and methods explained in
this unique book, which is called *"Money For the*

Taking" was the inspiration that caused a Chicago man to give up his job, raise $50,000 capital, and start a business of his own. From three small offices, the business grew, in less than 12 months' time to a point where it occupied the entire floor of a large office building, employing a large corps of workers—and netting its owner over $5000 a month profit.

A woman who read *"Money for the Taking,"* who had had no previous business experience was inspired to borrow a few hundred dollars and start a tea room of her own. This tea room is filled to capacity daily and this woman is making a handsome profit monthly.

A man right here in Brooklyn, who for years has been a salaried employee, and whom I let read the manuscript before the book was printed, was inspired to start a mail order business in his spare time, from which he is netting weekly double the amount of his salary. He will soon give up his job and devote his entire time to his own business.

A stenographer who for years had not made over $20.00 a week was able to secure a position as secretary to the head of an advertising agency at a salary of $50.00 weekly. She states that if she had not read *"Money for the Taking"* she would have been afraid to even apply for this job.

A New York business man says that a single reading gave him an idea from which he has already made $2500, with much more in the offing.

I could give you many other instances like this,

(Names and addresses on request.) But it is only from an actual examination and a careful reading of the book itself that you can realize the vital importance of the message it contains and the dynamic urge to achievement which it inspires in the reader.

Please read the enclosed folder which describes *"Money for the Taking"* more fully, and which will give you at least a partial idea of the contents of this amazing book, written by a man who is not a theorist but who has himself demonstrated the practicability of his ideas and methods through his own large earnings.

But *"Money for the Taking"* is its own best spokesman. Read the enclosed circular through carefully—then accept at once the special offer which I have made you. Realize that in accepting my offer you take absolutely no risk whatsoever. Remember, you have an entire week to read the book and decide for yourself just how important a message it contains—a message which may easily make 1947 the most important year of your life.

Now (while the year is yet young) is the time for you to lay your foundation for bigger money, greater fun in living and the happiness and satisfaction which comes from personal independence and financial security.

In replying please be sure to use the order blank and the return envelope enclosed for your convenience.

Very sincerely,

* * *

You can see from this letter how readily any new idea could be presented to your prospective customers, and how appealing it would sound to them. Many a mail order fortune has been started on just such a letter as that. It is my hope to be able to show you in this Course of Lessons how you *may* start such a fortune.

LESSON V

THE POWER OF A STRONG APPEAL

What is the first essential in starting a business of your own today?

Ask nine out of ten people that, and they will tell you—*Capital!*

"If I only had the capital," sighs the average young man. "I know a business that would mint a barrel of money in no time."

But no one is sufficiently impressed to offer him the capital, so he goes through the years bemoaning the fact that he never had a chance.

Imagine what such a man would say if you offered him $23.00 and told him to start his business on that! "Chicken feed," he would probably call it, and tell you the day was past when big business could be built on such foundations.

Yet $23.00 was all Bruce Haughton had when he decided to start an automotive business in Jacksonville, Florida.

With $14.40 of his capital he bought some tools. Then he rented the 2-car garage in the back yard of the house where he had secured a room, and set up his sign.

He didn't depend upon the sign, however, to bring in the business. He figured that *he* was the only one who could do that. So he called upon a number of professional men and told them of the personal service he could give their cars which they couldn't get elsewhere. In odd moments during the next few weeks, he continued these calls, and thereafter he used letters and postcards to tell more people about his distinctive service.

At the end of the first thirty days, he had a net return from his investment of money, work, and brains of $476.80, with an overhead expense of only $50!

That was in the spring. By June, he found he had to have bigger quarters, for 591 regular customers were already coming to his "Backyard Garage" for service they could not buy elsewhere.

In the following February, he had to move again. This time to a corner in one of the best parts of the city.

A year later, he moved a third time, closer by five blocks to the business section, within easy reach of the big office buildings where the bigger part of his clientele was located and *ten times as big as his first place!*

Not only that, but he started a Motor Club that soon had fifty branch garages all over Florida and Georgia. In these garages his products were sold, his name became known, his services was talked about.

And all on a capital of $23.00! The next time someone tells you all the things he would do if a rich aunt would die and leave him a million, show him this. Tell him he *has* the only capital that is necessary to start any worthy enterprise. An idea, and the brains and energy to push it.

Today Bruce Haughton is the head of an Advertising Agency in Jacksonville, an agency that specializes in helping different firms with their sales promotion. To quote from a recent letter from Mr. Haughton— "I recently completed a period of training of men in the George A. Hormel Company, Austin, Minnesota, where I put into effect a sales campaign that is now being used nationally on their product SPAM. The results of this sales idea showed net sales increases of 23% in Minnesota and Wisconsin in the first 12 weeks of operation. Just what the increase has been since then I do not know, but they are using full page newspaper spreads to announce the program through-out the country."

Pick up almost any magazine and you will find an advertisement of the Wilson Chemical Co., Tyrone, Pennsylvania. They offer premiums to agents selling their "Coversine" Salve. This business was started by Mr. George C. Wilson in a most unusual way. He learned of a formula for a salve that sounded as though it had sales possibilities. He got the details immediately. Working at night and in spare time, he started his business. For several years, his factory was the kitchen stove and his office the kitchen table. As sales increased, he rented quarters to increase his manufacturing facilities. Today, the Wilson Chemical Co. occupies a modern plant and has thousands of agents all over the world. From this one product alone, Mr. Wilson has made a fortune. All he had to start with was a formula and a good sales idea.

In one of their circulars, *Popular Mechanics* told how a chap by the name of Robert Rauth conceived the idea of making a shampoo for blondes exclusively, one that would keep blonde hair golden always restore the golden beauty to faded unlovely blonde hair. He experimented with a formula, tried it out with friends, sold himself on this product, and then got in touch with an advertising agency. The agency liked the idea and formed a company to manufacture the product. The company never had a salesman. All sales came from the advertising which drove worried blondes into the drug stores. "Blondex" sales were as high as $500,000 a year. Right now they probably run $300,000 a year. The product has a relatively small market, being for use of blondes only, (20% of women are blondes). Yet, look at the money this man made. He started with only a formula and an idea.

But did you *ever* hear the inside story of how F. W. Fitch, originator of Fitch's Ideal Dandruff Remover, built a million dollar business with only $45.00 capital?

This story is so fascinating that I believe you will find it interesting, too. Let me tell you about it, as given by *Popular Mechanics.*

When F. W. Fitch was a young man in Iowa, he contracted a disease known as "scald-head." As a result, he lost most of his hair. In trying to locate the cause of the trouble, he became interested in the barber trade and bought the O. K. Barber Shop in Boone, Iowa.

Even though the barber shop Mr. Fitch bought was in a small town, he made a net profit of $1,200 as a barber during the first six months he operated the shop. While studying the cause of "scald-head," he worked out the formula for Fitch's Ideal Dandruff Remover. The patrons of his shop were the first to use the new product. It brought results. Other barber shops in Boone tried Fitch's Ideal Dandruff Remover and they, too, were enthusiastic about it. The news spread. In a few months, barbers in nearby towns were ordering supplies from Fitch.

This gave Fitch another idea. Why not go into the barber supply business and furnish tonics, shampoos, lotions, shaving creams and kindred products? And so Fitch decided to add other products to his line.

In the beginning, Mr. Fitch made up the merchandise personally. He demonstrated his products at barber shops. He was his own sales-man. After he would sell an order, he would hurry home to make up the merchandise. Progress at first was slow and tedious. For years, Fitch could not even afford to hire anyone to help him. Today, the F.W. Fitch Company has twenty-five salesmen calling on the barber trade and eight salesmen handling the drug and department store trade.

Fitch products are used now in over 75,000 barber shops and 20,000 beauty parlors. The annual sales run well over a million dollars. The Fitch plant is humming with activity.

But Fitch's success is not unusual. Many a profitable business has been built with only a formula and limited capital. George Eastman, the inventor of the Kodak, made millions and he started with nothing more than a formula for coating photographic plates. Helena Rubinstein, Polish girl, began in a small way as a beauty specialist with her own formulas for beauty preparations, and made $100,000 before she was twenty. Vick's Vapo-Rub was originated in the back room of a little store. In one year alone, over 30 million jars of Vick's were sold. John D. Larkin, famous soap manufacturer, started by making soap in his kitchen. Charles Post, who amassed a fortune of $20,000,000 began by making his "Postum" in small quantities and peddling it, himself. Milo Jones, owner of a large sausage business, was originally just a farmer with some pigs and a good recipe for sausage. He made a fortune.

You have probably tasted some of the delicious Mary Elizabeth candies, but do you know how they were started? Their story is the story of Mary Elizabeth Evans, who at one time was the youngest business woman in America.

The Evans family lived in Syracuse, New York. Their grandfather had been a judge and was looked upon as a wealthy man. Certainly he had a great deal of property, but the bulk of it consisted of a hundred small houses at one end of the city, and two or three shops. All were mortgaged to a greater or lesser extent, just as most property is today. But in the hands of a successful business man like the grandfather, those mortgages were easily carried.

Mary Elizabeth's father died, however, and when the grandfather in turn passed on, he left Mary Elizabeth's mother little or no cash, only this great bulk of mortgaged property which no woman, unaccustomed to business methods, could have been expected to carry. The result was that the mortgages were foreclosed, and Mrs. Evans found herself without property and with only $300 left in the bank.

Quite a change from her former life as a prospective heiress to a rich estate. Add to it the fact that she had three young daughters to provide for, the oldest only 14, and you can appreciate the problem that stared her in the face. That she and her girls found the solution to it so promptly and so successfully is as great a tribute to the courage and resource of American womanhood as one can find.

The oldest of the three daughters, Mary Elizabeth, had always been fond of making candy, and her delicious home-made sweets were the envy of every girl of her acquaintance. When the family fortunes reached such low ebb, the thought naturally occurred to her—if everyone loved these candies so much when she served them at parties *free,* wouldn't they like them just as well if they had to pay for them? She decided to try.

But, as she wisely reasoned, the reason people had liked them so well was because they were made from the best ingredients; thick cream, the best butter, fresh nuts, rich chocolate, and pure maple sugar. If they were to enjoy the candies she offered for sale, these candies must be made of just as rich ingredients, regardless of cost.

When the exchequer is down to $300 and there's nothing more in sight, it takes courage to lay out part of that $300 on the most expensive ingredients for an unknown market. But Mary Elizabeth made up the first pound of candy to sell, made it more carefully, more "deliciously" than any she had ever prepared for a party, and upon the box, in her own hand, she wrote, "Mary Elizabeth's home-made candy," then sent the box to an informal gathering of grown people.

That little sample brought her orders the next day for six more boxes. And those six orders were the beginning of the Mary Elizabeth Candy Kitchen.

When she made them, she made other sample boxes to send to friends and acquaintances and social gatherings. The orders steadily grew, and with them grew her ability to handle them. Each member of the family—Mary Elizabeth, her mother and the two younger girls— took over some allotted part of the work. Each did her best to carry out the one idea that these candies must be made just as they had been aforetime, when there was plenty of money, plenty of time, and only the palate and the joy of making to be considered.

With an objective such as that, business could not help but grow. The demand among friends and acquaintances became so great that Mary Elizabeth felt they should start a little store. The time of all four was so fully occupied, however, that none could be spared to attend store, so they conceived the happy idea of starting a "Help Yourself" store. A booth was set up under the stairway in the University Building in Syracuse, with this sign upon it—

> "Open these doors
> Take what you will
> Leave cost of goods taken
> Make your change from my till."

Only a child or an inexperienced business woman would show such sublime faith in people's honesty. And only one with such faith could put all people so upon their honor. The "Help Yourself" booth was an immediate success. And in all the time it ran, there was only one theft. Can greater tribute be paid to the innate honesty of human nature, or the unswerving faith of childhood? It was as fine a proof as could be asked of the old adage that "to the pure all things are pure," for no one not meticulously honest herself would ever have thought of trusting so fully in the honesty of others.

Naturally, the business grew and prospered. Naturally, it moved on to larger quarters. It was not long till the Tea Room on Fifth Avenue in New York was opened, which is now the headquarters of Mary Elizabeth's candy.

Of course, as the business grew, Mary Elizabeth could no longer continue to make the candy herself. Her time was needed for management and direction. But her guiding hand, and that of her mother and others, is as evident in the delicious product of today, as in the first batch turned out. The kitchen is still as spotless, the ingredients as rich, and the formulas those which Mary Elizabeth and her mother and sisters have worked out.

For those who would like to emulate the wonderful work she has done, Mary Elizabeth has written a book containing these formulas, called "My Candy Secrets."

Perhaps you have seen the postcard offering a 5-lb. bag of peanuts for $1.90, which one man used to start a profitable mail order business. In the beginning, he wrote them with pen and ink, by hand, and mailed them to the parents of growing youngsters, where he felt sure there would be a good demand for peanuts. As the orders came in, and he began to get money ahead, he had his hand-written cards reproduced by printing, so that they still looked as though he had written them himself. Here is the way they read.

* * *

Here's a treat for you

I want to send you *at my risk and expense* a 5-pound bag of Delicious Redskin Brand Peanuts. Big, choice, full-flavored nuts, the Cream of the Virginia crop, and already shelled for you.

After you and the family have eaten your fill if you find them satisfactory you may send me your check for $1.90. If you don't think they're the finest peanuts you ever tasted, send the remainder back to me within 3 days, and you won't owe me a cent.

If this appeals to you as a fair proposition and to

your appetite for "honest to goodness" *Big* peanuts, fresh from Sunny Virginia write "Send me a bag" and sign your name on the face of this card and then mail it back to:

Yours for a feast

John Jones

* * *

Frank E. Davis of Gloucester used the same method. Here is one of the pieces of copy he found most effective:

* * *

Dear Mrs. ......

Have you any objection to my putting a pail of choice Salt Mackerel in your home for you to try? Then, some morning soon, have one of these splendid fish broiled for breakfast with plenty of melted butter and baked potatoes.

After that, if you feel that this delicious breakfast isn't worth repeating, if your folks will let you do it, you can send back the unused portion of the pail, and your breakfast will have been "on me."

If you'd like to make this test at my risk, just fill in the enclosed card and mail at once.

Very truly yours,

* * *

Most people would say that fish would be hard to sell by mail it is so easy to get them fresh at the nearest market. Yet Davis has sold as much as $2,000,000 worth in a single year. And lest you think such an offer must be high-powered salesmanship, I give you below copy of one of the letters he used very successfully. As you see, it is just the sort of simple, homely letter anyone might write, and therein lies its pulling power. People are willing to believe that a man who writes this simply may be an authority on fish, from the very fact that he doesn't pretend to know anything about advertising or letter writing:

* * *

Dear Friend:

There's no use trying. I've tried and tried to tell people about my fish. But I wasn't rigged out to be a letter writer, and I can't do it. I can close-haul a sail with the best of them. I know how to pick out the best fish of the catch, I know just which fish will make the tastiest mouthfuls, but I'll never learn the knack of writing a letter that will tell people why my kind of fish, fresh-caught prime grades, right off the fishing boats with the deep-sea tang still in it, is lots better than the ordinary store kind.

But if I can't explain it, at least you can taste the difference. So you won't mind, will you, if I ship some of my fish direct to your home. It won't cost you anything. All I ask is that you try the fish at my expense and judge for yourself whether it isn't exactly what you have always wanted.

I've made up a Special Get-Acquainted Assortment to let people know how good my fish are. You see, I can tell people that I give them the first pick of the finest, primest catches. But the best way to let them know that my fish is exactly what I say, is to send a generous, meal-size sample so they can taste how good my fish is. That's just what you get in my Get-Acquainted Assortment; fourteen different varieties of delicious seafoods, that will tell you as no fine writing ever can, what a real treat it is to eat fish shipped straight to your home from the fishing smacks.

For nearly 40 years I have been doing just this, selecting the primest grades of ocean fish to be sent direct from the fishing boats to my customers. And it is real pride I feel to know that over 150,000 families have found my fish so much better than any they could get locally that season in and season out they send me their orders.

Today I invite you to join them. I want you to know the rich, satisfying taste of fresh-caught, prime-grade seafood. If you have never tasted anything but the kind you get in stores, there's a rare treat awaiting you. Read the postal card enclosed and see how you can get this offer without risking a penny in advance. All you do now is to fill in the card, and your seafoods will be on the way to you the very day I hear from you. You pay nothing, unless you're perfectly satisfied that my fish really are the best.

It is just this way that I secured my 150,000 customers. So you know beforehand that you can send your order with full confidence. You know in advance that you will get the choicest, tenderest, fullest-flavored seafood that you've ever tasted. Check and sign the post card and mail it to me,

TODAY.

Very truly yours,

* * *

All over the country, similar offers are being made. From out in Washington you can get a special kind of Oyster by mail. From down in Florida, you get the famous Pompano. From Baltimore, Delane Brown offers you Shad at $4.75 for a dozen fillets. And here is the way he fully justifies that seemingly high price.

* * *

Dear Friend:

May I send you, to try AT MY RISK, something that many people have told me is the FINEST seafood delicacy they have ever tasted?

I believe, and I hope you will agree, there is no fish with a richer, more delicate flavor than the Chesapeake Bay SHAD. Truly it would be our most popular fish if it were not for the tiny bones that are so hard to remove except by methods known only to skilled chefs.

At Miller Brothers' nationally famous restaurant in Baltimore, during the short fresh shad season, boneless shad fillets are a popular seafood dish at $1.00 per serving. In uptown Baltimore the Walker-Hasslinger seafood restaurant serves broiled boneless shad at 90 cents an order. Thousands of Baltimoreans and visitors to the city gladly pay these prices to enjoy this outstanding fish for which the Chesapeake Bay region is noted.

Yet you can serve the same delicious dish in your own home at any time and at less than one-third of these prices. For I have found a way to make shad a year around treat and with the annoyance of the many small bones completely removed. Etc.

* * *

From Maine and Vermont many people are now selling maple sugar candies and syrup by mail. From other places, fruit cakes, hams, sausages, and a hundred other products are being successfully marketed by mail. Even fresh eggs and fresh-killed chickens are profitably sold his way.

No matter what your product, no matter where you are located, here is nearly always a way of reaching your possible customers with an appeal that will touch their appetites or their desires, and open their pocketbooks. In succeeding lessons, we shall show you exactly how different ones have done this and how you may do the same.

LESSON VI

THE LAW OF SOWING AND REAPING

Do you know what is the oldest law in the world? Do you know what law was considered so important that it was repeated no less than six times in the very first chapter of Genesis, and referred to scores of times throughout the Scriptures?

The Law that everything reproduces after its kind. What ye sow, that shall ye also reap. In Eastern countries, it is called the Law of Karma, of "Come back."

So logical is this law that you wonder at anyone who expects it to work otherwise. You would not sow corn and expect to reap wheat. You would not plant potatoes and expect to harvest onions. Yet many a man plants seeds of selfishness, of dishonesty and greed, and expects to reap from them a harvest of riches, happiness and success!

Life does not work that way. "Do men gather grapes of thorns, or figs from thistles?" asked Jesus. If we want the good things of life, we must sow seeds of good, no matter on how small a scale we have to start. Take any successful man or business, and you will find that success based on some worthwhile service.

Henry Ford is said to have been offered a billion dollars for the Ford Motor Company. He refused it. Not because he wanted more than that, a billion is more money than any one man can use, more than he wants to leave to his children—but because the Ford Motor Company was Henry Ford's means of rendering service to his fellow man. Take that away from him, and you'd have taken most of his reason for living.

"Those who bring happiness into the lives of others," said Barrie, "cannot keep it from themselves." And the same is true of any other good thing you bring into the lives of others. Give of what you have, and as you give, so will it come back to you.

You see, whatever you give, of good or evil, must first pass through you. And you become tinged with it. To bring evil into the lives of others means bringing it to yourself as well, for you must first draw it to you before you can give it to them. To give good to them is to bring it into your own life too.

So don't be afraid of giving too great value for the money you get. What you give over and above that which is justly due, serves as seeds of fortune, seeds which will bring you increase at harvest time just as surely as the wheat you sow in the spring brings a crop in the fall.

> "I shall pass through this world but once.
> Any good thing therefore that I can do,
> Or any kindness that I can show to any human being,
> Let me do it now. Let me not defer it or neglect it,
> For I shall not pass this way again."

That is good neighborliness, but it is much more than that, too. It is good insurance as well. The man who never misses a chance to do good to others will find, one of these days, that others are just as anxious to do good to him. Chickens come home to roost. Happy is the man whose chickens are the kind that he can welcome home, whose seeds bring back to him crops of happiness and contentment.

In a rural community out on the Pacific Coast, there lived two brothers who had just fallen heir to an old pear orchard. Years before, their father had planted an orchard of Comys Pears. These pears are large and juicy and very sweet, but the trees do not start to bear commercially until they are about twenty years old, so few farmers have the patience or the capital to cultivate them.

When these two boys (whom we shall call the Smith Brothers, because that was not their name) inherited the orchard, the only method they knew of selling their pears was to ship them to the commission merchants in the big cities, and let them sell them for what they would bring, remitting the balance after paying freight and commission.

That balance was pitiably small. Even though their pears brought a premium over all ordinary kinds, the commission merchants could not be expected to go out of their way to find special markets for them, with the result that some years the two brothers got barely enough for their crop to pay the expenses of cultivation.

So they put their heads together, and decided that since no one else would find a special market for their pears, it was up to them to do it themselves. They picked a few boxes of especially large juicy and delicious pears, and shipped them to the heads of substantial business concerns, at the same time writing them a letter asking them to TRY the pears, and if they liked them, order a number of boxes as gifts for their business friends and associates.

That experiment pulled so well that they decided to try to sell ALL their pears by mail. First, they put advertisements of their pears in likely magazines, like the GIFT Columns of *House Beautiful, House & Garden* and the like. Then they picked lists of people who had bought other products by mail, and to them they sent letters along the lines of the following.

* * *

Would You Be Good Enough to Do Me a Favor?

You Can Help to Solve a Problem of Importance!

Dear Sir:

Though I have never met you, I am writing to you

as one man to another. You can help me to make an important decision, and I don't think you will mind doing it when I explain. I know I would gladly do as much for you, if you asked me.

With this letter, I am sending you a folder that tells about the rarest fruit grown in America, one of the rarest in all the world, a pear so big and juicy that you have to eat it with a spoon, so delicious and tasty that it is served in the finest hotels and restaurants of Paris and London at about 75 cents each!

I refer to Smith Brothers' Pears.

Smith Brothers' Pears came originally from the south of France. They can be grown in only a few select spots where the rich soil and gentle rains and days on end of glorious sunshine coax them to their mammoth size, gorgeous beauty and delicious flavor. Few are willing to take the chance of cultivating them, however, for they not only require expert care, but they do not bear commercially *until the trees are twenty years old!*

That is why their fruit is so rare. That is why it commands such high prices abroad, where it has been looked upon for generations back as the most delicious fruit grown, and where it has graced the tables of Czars and Kings, as well as of all who aspired to distinction in their viands and their taste.

But there are people of discriminating taste in this country, too. So my brother Harry and I have been making an experiment. Instead of shipping all of our Smith Brothers' Pears to Europe, we have, in the past couple of years, been putting aside some of this luscious, golden fruit, rare as orchids, honey sweet and bursting with juice, for use as gifts at Christmas time from business men to those whom they wanted to remember with a distinctive treat, a thrilling surprise quite outside the ordinary commonplace run of gifts.

You can judge of the enthusiasm with which those gifts were received when I tell you that Mrs. So-and-So of Palm Beach wrote us that thereafter she would use no other pears in her household, and Mrs. So-and-so ordered a box *every two weeks during the season!*

Which brings me to the reason for this letter: The number of pears we put aside last year for use in this country is not going to be nearly enough this year. So I'd like to determine in advance, if I can, how many boxes I am going to need here, and cut down my commitments abroad by that much. Otherwise, I am going to have a lot of disappointed friends here.

Will you give me the benefit of your judgment? Will you look over the enclosed folder, and tell me if YOU have any friends that you would like to remember with a real surprise treat this Christmas?

The Manager of the Blank Hotel in San Francisco gave some to different guests last year, and he wrote us, "In all my years of experience, I have never given presents so popular with my resident guests."

If you would like to give some of your friends or

business associates the most thrilling surprise they have known for many a long day, if you would like to send them at Christmas a gift so different from the usual commonplace gifts of cigars or liquor or fountain pens or whatnot, that they will remember it and the donor pleasurably throughout the year, use the enclosed order form NOW!

"Words simply cannot express the delight of our friends in receiving this delicious fruit," wrote the President of one of the big Motion Picture companies. And that is what your friends will be telling you if you use the enclosed form now to order some of these luscious pears for them this Christmas.

Yet the price is less than you would pay for many an ordinary gift. Only $1.98 for the standard size 10-lb. box and $2.98 for the large size Family box. And the pears will come to them, tissue wrapped, nestled in cushion packing in handsome gift boxes, and bearing your greeting card, by express *charges pre paid.*

A more delightful gift would be hard to imagine, or one that has in the past two years called forth such heartfelt appreciation on the part of recipients. There are only a few still available for this year's gifts. If you want even a glimpse of this delicious, golden, rarest of all fruits, if you want to give to a few friends the thrilling surprise treat of their lives, it is essential that you mail the enclosed order form NOW!

Sincerely,

* * *

Those advertisements and letters pulled. They pulled so well that in a few years, the two brothers were selling ALL their pears by mail at a nice profit. They pulled so well that all the orchardists in their alley got together and marketed their Comys Pears through these two brothers. Last year, they sold more than 80,000 boxes of pears by mail!

But in the nature of things, fresh pears can be sold at only one season of the year, in the late Fall and early Winter. And once they ad built up so profitable a list of customers, it seemed too bad not to be cashing in on it all through the year. So the Smith Brothers started to look around for other fruits of distinctive size and flavor that they might offer to their customers at different times of the year. Presently they came across nectarines of superb quality, big black grapes that might readily pass for the hot-house variety, peaches so big and juicy that they rivaled their pears for flavor.

Then to their list of customers they sent a letter like this:

***

I Wonder If You Will Be Good Enough
To help Us Make An Important Decision?

Dear Customer

Right now my brother and I are selecting the rare fruits that are to go during the next year to the members of our "Rare Fruit Club," to those who have bought our Smith Brothers' Pears, and who have asked us to find them other luscious fruits of a similar quality. This would cover only fruits of the most unusual character, extra choice as to size and flavor—the kind that most people never even see.

In our search for such exotic and delicious fruits,

we have discovered a California orchard that grows the huge, flaming Nectarines that you find occasionally in the finest fruit stores.

This orchard is so jealous of the reputation of its Nectarines for unique flavor and delicious quality that it makes a point of delivering them *fresh from the tree* to exclusive hotels and fruit shops.

Perhaps you have never eaten a fresh, *tree-ripened* Nectarine of this extra choice quality? If not, you have yet to enjoy a rare and delectable taste experience. It is one that few ever enjoy, because these Nectarines are in season for only 20 days beginning about July 25th. At other times, they have to be imported from abroad. Our representative was in New York a few weeks ago, and the price asked for Belgian Nectarines at the finest fruit shop was $25.00 a dozen!

The top grade of this California orchard's Nectarines is superior to any imported from abroad, but at the height of the season, it sells in fine fruit shops for only $1.25 a dozen. A lovelier fruit would be hard to find. It has the most delicate taste and magnificent aroma of anything in the whole fruit kingdom. It is the highest priced fruit sold in England. During its short season here, the fruit is picked in the early mornings, packed carefully and then rushed immediately to refrigerator protection to protect its full, fresh, delicate flavor.

Now, here is our problem: We must decide whether these delicious, big fresh Nectarines would be appreciated by enough people to justify including them as one of the rare fruits going to our Club Members.

Will you help us to make the decision? We should greatly appreciate it if you would. And to show our appreciation, we have arranged with the grower to make up a special box of 30 to 35 of these tree-ripened, marvelously delicious Nectarines. In fruit stores, this large size sells for 10 cents each. But if you will help by giving us the benefit of your opinion, we will send a box of extra choice size and flavor to you, tree-ripened, fresh and luscious all express charges prepaid for little more than half the store price, only $1.98. Your name on the attached special order form will bring them to you.

You know what it is to enjoy the kind of rare fruits that the average person never even has a chance to buy, for you have had our Smith Brothers' Pears in the past. There's another treat coming to you when first you bite into a big, tree-ripened Nectarine. Last year, a good many customers who know that our Pears can be shipped only during a short winter season wrote to ask whether we could not tell them where they could get other rare fruits of a like unusual quality during the early months of the Fall.

It was not easy to find what our customers asked for, because we knew they were looking only for fruits that might equal in character and quality our own Smith Brothers' Pears. But in two other places we did find exactly what we had hoped for. One grower makes a specialty of mammoth tree-ripened Peaches, the biggest, juiciest peaches you ever saw, so big, in fact, that just one is a handful. When they are ripe, they are fairly bursting with juice. The crop will be at its peak of full, rich firmness in time to ship in September, just after Labor Day.

That was one find. Another was the famous vineyard that grows the choicest big, black Grapes. Harry and I had some these last Fall, and we agreed that they were the biggest, choicest and sweetest Grapes we had ever seen or tasted. Most this year's limited crop will go to hotels in London, Paris and New York, but we have arranged for a limited number of boxes for the members of our "Rare Fruit Club" when these marvelous Grapes are ready for shipment in October, and if speak for them now, I think we may still get a few more.

In November, of course, our own Smith Brothers' Pears will be ready to ship, and this year I think our crop is going be the finest we have ever had. You know what Smith Brothers Pears are, so I don't need to tell you anything about their aroma or their luscious, juicy sweetness.

Now here is our special offer. If we have word from you NOW, we can ship to you in July, in September, in October and in November, a big box each month of rare and delicious fruits, as follows:

In July—box of huge flaming Nectarines

In September—box of Mammoth Peaches

In October—box of big black Grapes

In November—box of Smith Brothers' Pears

All will be shipped by express, *charges prepaid,* and the cost of all four will be, NOT the high price you would pay in hotels or fine fruit stores, BUT

ONLY $7.95 for all four boxes! If you should want to order only the Nectarines now, the price of them alone is $1.98 a box, express prepaid.

Can you imagine a more distinctive remembrance for relatives or friends, than these four surprise boxes? Can you think of a greater thrill than to get one of them each month at your own home, for your own family? Or you might give pleasure to four different friends by ordering one box for each of them.

Here's all you need to do. Send us on the enclosed form the names of those you want to remember with this unusual treat, enclose check or money order for $7.95 for each 4-box order and we'll do the rest. We'll promise that each box of these rare fruits will be packed with the utmost care and shipped to arrive in perfect condition.

And here's our guarantee: If, after trying the first box, you are not more than satisfied, just return what is left of it and we'll refund your money in full and cancel the rest of your order.

That's fair enough, you'll agree. But if you are like So and So, you will be ordering more instead of canceling Mrs. So and So wrote us, (Here fill in testimonial).

One thing, though, you must not overlook. There's no time to delay if you want those delicious tree ripened Nectarines. Their entire season lasts only 20 days, and that season starts July 25th. The crop is unusually limited this year, and so great is the demand for the big, luscious Nectarines grown by this one orchard that we were able to reserve only a comparatively few boxes. If you want a chance at them, it would be well to mail your order right away.

Sincerely,

Smith Brothers,

Smith Brothers Orchards,

City   State

Please send, express prepaid, to each name and address listed below your special 4-box series of rare fruits—

In July—box of huge, flaming Nectarines

In September—box of Mammoth Peaches

In October—box of big black Grapes

In November—box of Smith Brothers' Pears

At $7.95 for each complete series, I enclose check or money order for $_____ in full payment.

Please enclose in each box gift card signed:

Sign Your Name Here

Street

City   State

Check here if you wish to order the Nectarines alone. Our Special price to you on them is $1.98 a box, *express prepaid.*

* * *

So successful was this offer that the Smith Brothers now have more than 10,000 customers who order from four to eight different kinds of fruits from them by mail. Even during the winter months, when there are no fresh fruits available, they are able to sell these people boxes of home-made preserves, candies and the like. They have sold them candies, spices, artificial flowers, Christmas decorations, honey, tea, spices, apples, oranges, black Mission Figs. In fact, I don't believe there is a product they have offered to this list that has not brought back profitable returns. Naturally, some products have a much greater appeal than others, so they specialize on those that pull best, but once you have built a list of this kind; there is hardly a thing you can offer them that they will not buy in reasonable quantity.

Here, for instance, is a letter on Seckel pears:

* * *

Once in a Blue Moon—
There Comes a Chance Like This!

Dear Customer:
Remember, as a youngster, how you used to love those small, sweet Seckel Pears? Remember how good they tasted, how many of them you were able to put away?

Imagine those same pears, twice as big, twice as juicy and many times as sweet. Wouldn't you enjoy a few of them right now?

The ordinary small Seckel Pear is grown in New

England and New York State. But out here in our Valley, where the rich soil and the gentle rains and the weeks on end of glorious sunshine all work together to make it the finest Pear country in the world, we grow a special variety of Seckel Pear that is considered by Connoisseurs to be second in flavor to none.

We call these special Seckels "Small Sweets" because they are only half the size of "Smith Brothers' Pears," but even at that, they are twice as big as the Eastern grown Seckel—twice as tasty and delicious, too. Incidentally, they bring nearly three times the price, in the New York Market, of Bartlett Pears!

The entire crop of these "Small Sweets" amounts to only about half a dozen carloads, and it is all shipped now. But just as an experiment, we saved out 500 boxes to see how our customers like them. While they last, you can get them, EXPRESS PREPAID, for $1.98 a box.

They carry this guarantee. If, after trying them, you are not more than satisfied, send them back and we will refund your $1.98 at once and in full.

I am not trying to hurry you, but we really did save out only 500 boxes for this experiment, so if you want any, it would be well to mail your order today. Better still, AIR MAIL it—for we shall have to make it—"First come, first served!"

Sincerely,

* * *

The same type of letter might be used to offer apples, figs, dates or any other fruit. The problem, of course, is to build your customer list. To do that, take the product that has the strongest appeal and the widest margin of profit. Offer it in a small unit to begin with, say $1.00, $1.98 or $2.98. Here is the way it was done with Santa Clara Valley Figs, as reported in one of the mail order magazines.

* * *

Dear Mr. McPherson:

May I send you, on approval, a ten-pound box of delicious Santa Clara Valley figs at a fraction of the price you would pay for them at Park & Tilford's or any store handling delicacies?

Figs, as you know, are one of the most healthful foods that you can eat. Along with a delicious flavor, Nature has stored in them certain essential food elements especially needed at this season.

Let me send you a box or more of these big, tender figs, the pick of the Santa Clara Valley, with the understanding that you need not pay for them unless you are more than pleased. The price is $3.00 plus parcel post for figs; $2.75 for equal quality prunes.

After you receive the figs, you will probably find that your friends and neighbors will want to know where you bought them, and if they too, can secure a box. We will be glad to include a complimentary box of prunes, with a pooled order for ten boxes of figs.

Don't miss this treat. The opportunity to get a complimentary box of big, delicious Santa Clara Valley prunes. You may send your check with order, or we will send the figs C.O.D. as you prefer. There is an order blank enclosed.

Very truly yours,

* * *

In the same magazine was given another letter, offering preserved figs at a much higher price. Both letters were excellently done and from the report given of them, brought back highly profitable returns. Here is the second letter.

* * *

Dear Friend:

Do you like those delicious, big, skinless preserved figs that are served in dining cars and clubs at 40 cents a portion? Would you like to get some of the same figs at a price that is only a fraction of what you paid before?

Figs, as you know, are one of the most healthful foods you can eat. Along with delicious flavor, Nature has stored in them certain essential food elements especially needed at this season.

Served just as they are in the rich syrup, these preserved figs of mine are a delightful breakfast dish. Topped with cream, either plain or whipped, it would be hard to find a more delicious, yet wholesome dessert. Just imagine a dish of ice cream smothered with a sauce made of these figs minced in their syrup.

So-and-So of Detroit, Michigan, says of them, "That case of figs is worth more than a case of medicine," while C. W. of Roanoke, Virginia, writes, "These figs are just what I have been looking for."

If you would like to try these figs that others like so well, I will gladly send you, at my risk and expense, a case containing two dozen 13-oz. tins of the finest figs grown; big, plump, delicious and tender.

When the case reaches you, open a can, let the whole family try them as a breakfast dish or dessert. Then if you want to keep them, just send me your check for $7.60 to cover the entire shipment. If you don't think these are the finest figs you ever tasted, return the rest to me and you won't owe me a cent.

Don't miss this real treat. Just sign the enclosed card, mail it to me. I will ship the box the same day your order reaches me.

Yours for good health,

* * *

And here is another letter on Pears from David J. Elliott of Courtland, California, and he writes one of the most interesting letters we have ever been privileged to read. His pears are expensive, but note with what cleverness he builds up a picture of value, a picture which makes their price seem comparatively small.

The background he manages to paint in, the traditions of quality he implies, the flattery he extends to his prospects, all this is artistry. Observe the import of his closing three words: "We never substitute."

* * *

$20.67 for a single pear!

Here at Stillwater Orchard we have a small block of ancient pear trees that yield the world's most precious fruit.

Not that we get $20.67 per pear these days—but we did in Uncle David's time.

Uncle David came to California in the 1850's, attracted by gold, of course. But he never did get to the "diggings," because he fell in love with the quiet beauty and rich, black soil of the Sacramento River Delta.

During the gold rush any farmer was a freak in California, but Uncle David was considered completely insane. Instead of following the lead of the few who did turn the virgin soil and plant wheat, he sent to France for pear trees!

Ten thousand miles they came, across the Atlantic, around the Horn and up the Pacific. In 1860 they arrived and Stillwater Orchard was planted.

These pears were soon famous and when the old steam-wheel river boats pulled up to Stillwater Landing the miners would start shouting their bids before the paddles stopped turning. It wasn't at all unusual for the price to get to an ounce of gold for a single pear, $20.67 in those days.

Uncle David's rare French pears were always superb, but today they are truly without equal, for the older a pear tree grows, the finer the fruit it bears.

We have only 21 acres of these 78-year-old trees and I feel that their yield is too precious to offer in the usual markets. So now my father and I pack them in strikingly beautiful containers and offer them in limited edition to a very restricted clientele of connoisseurs.

You can pay no finer compliments than to send these pears as a business or personal gift; can enjoy no greater luxury than to order regular shipments for your own use. We guarantee that you will never be disappointed.

You will find more of the fascinating story of our pears on the pages within, plus an order form that we suggest mailing at once, for our season is short and the supply of these rare pears strictly limited. We never substitute.

Sincerely,

* * *

The big profit in selling products of this kind lies not in the single order, but in re-selling these customers so that they will buy additional boxes for themselves and larger quantities to give to their friends.

Most business men today give Christmas gifts to employees, to customers or to business associates, and they are continually on the lookout for something out of the ordinary in the way of gifts. Desk sets and fountain pens and key rings and the like have become too commonplace. If their gift is to be remembered, it must be something out of the ordinary. So if you can make your product stand out from the crowd, you will get orders around the Holiday time. Not in single boxes, but by the scores and even hundreds.

It does not matter what your product may be, so long as you can make it sufficiently desirable. I know one concern that gives every employee a dressed turkey at Thanksgiving and at Christmas. I know others that give fruit cakes, boxes of fruit, etc.

How do they decide what they shall give? Usually some executive has bought that particular product or had it given to him the previous Christmas, and was so pleased with it that he urged it upon the Big Boss. So it is not a matter of immediate selling. It is a matter of making long-time friends for your product.

Here is a letter that has been used successfully for years by one of the big Orange Growers in Florida. It brings orders for trial boxes, and the fine fruit he ships brings the repeats:

* * *

Dear Friend:

Oranges and grapefruit right off the tree!

If you have ever been in Florida and eaten fruit you picked from the tree, you will remember how good it tasted. You re-marked, "I never ate fruit like that before!" There is a real treat awaiting you if you have never eaten fruit fresh from the trees.

It is not necessary to make a trip to Florida to have on your table delicious fruit ripened by sunshine,

Nature's *way*. So-and-So's fresh picked fruit, sent to you by a combined fast steamer and express service, will taste like that you would eat from the tree if you were here. We can now ship to you or your friends who live near the port cities, a half box of fresh oranges and grapefruit, picked especially to fill your order, all charges prepaid, for $3.50. Our regular price for this box to inland points by all-rail express is $3.75.

With your permission we would like to ship you a half box of oranges and grapefruit at our own risk and expense. When the fruit arrives examine it carefully and eat generously of it. If you are not entirely satisfied, return the remainder promptly by express collect and you owe us nothing; otherwise send us your cheek within ten days.

Sign your name and complete shipping address on the enclosed card, which requires no stamp, and mail it today. Immediately upon receipt of your order the fruit will be picked, packed and shipped direct to you.

Sincerely,

* * *

Finally, here is a letter offering home-made preserves and jellies. The idea of it is readily adaptable to any product of the kitchen; to cakes and candies and cookies and the like.

* * *

DO YOU REMEMBER

Your boyhood days and the delicious preserves and jellies Mother used to be making about this time?

Remember, at preserving time, how there would always be a little left over, not enough jars or else, not enough preserves to quite fill the last one, so you'd get those leftovers at supper fresh from the kitchen? And remember how good those new preserves and jellies always tasted, full-flavored and ripe and juicy?

"Shucks, no such preserves or jellies nowadays," you say.

You're wrong.

For what was it that made Mother's preserves so good?

Wasn't it because she used only fully-ripened, mature fruit and berries, with pure cane sugar? Wasn't it because she cooked them carefully, so as to lose as little of the natural flavors as possible, then served them to you while they were fresh?

Those same choice fruits and berries, fresh from vine and orchard, go into the preserves and jellies you get from our Home Kitchen. They are just as carefully selected, packed when the fruit is in its prime, fully-ripened, sound and fragrant.

But modern science has given us help that Mother never dreamed of. It has shown us how to hold all the rich, ripe flavor of the mature fruit, how to keep it from running to *syrup,* how to preserve its distinctive qualities in a way impossible in Mother's day.

You see, her whole purpose in cooking fruit, to preserve it was to drive the sugar into the fruit. But cooking in an open kettle draws out the juice, so she had to keep on cooking until most of this evaporated and the syrup got thick. That made the fruit shrink and took away much of its savor.

Modern science, on the other hand, has found a way to drive the sugar into the fruit with *cold* instead of heat, making so little cooking necessary that the fruit loses practically none of its juices, keeping not only its size, but it rich, natural flavor. That is why the expert buyer always looks first at the size of the fruit or berries, and then notes whether the jar is all fruit, or mostly syrup.

And that is why the preserves from our Home Kitchen are so full of fruit and berries, full size, rich and luscious, with barely enough syrup to keep them moist and fresh. That is why the jellies are clear as crystal, free from sediment.

Will you TRY a jar of these freshly-made preserves and jellies from our Home Kitchen, if I send a "Sampler" case to you at my own risk and expense for a week's FREE TRIAL? Will you pick out the variety you like best? TRY it? Compare its flavor with that of home-made preserves you pay $1.00 a jar for in the best grocery stores and return the balance, express collect, if you don't think these the best you have ever tasted, bar none?

There will be two full 16-ounce jars of each of our six different varieties of Preserves, and two 8-ounce tumblers of each of our six kinds of Jelly; (24 jars in all) a shelf-full of goodies that will delight, you and your family for many a days to come.

"Enclosed find check for more of your most delicious preserves and jellies," wrote Dr. Jones of Jonesville, Virginia. "They are as good as you say, and could not be improved upon in my opinion."

Yet, their price is not 50 cents or $1.00 a jar. Not even the 36 cents a jar we have had to charge in other years. BUT LESS THAN 25 cents each, $5.95 for the full case of *24, delivered to you!*

Send no money. Just your name and address on the enclosed card will bring the "Sampler" case to you, prepaid, for a week's free examination and trial. Open up any jar you like. Use it! Let the whole family try it. THEN DECIDE! If they are not the best Preserves and Jelly you ever tasted, if for wholesomeness for flavor, for mellow, delicious taste you have ever found their equal, send back the rest. And owe us nothing.

On that basis, will you TRY these freshly-made Preserves and Jellies? On that distinct understanding, will you mail the enclosed card?

Sincerely,

* * *

In selling foods, remember that people want flavor and tastiness first, but you will get their order more readily if you can also suggest that your product has elements that make it good for them as well.

All of us are getting more and more health-conscious about our foods, but this is especially true of the mail order buyer. Your best mail order buyer is the man of middle age. He has reached the point where he has a little extra money that he can spend on himself, and he has begun to be concerned about his health or his failing vigor or vitality, if your product will help, even in a slight degree, to regain or retain these, and at the same time will appeal to his taste. You have a mail order item that you can build into a big and profitable business.

LESSON VII

WHAT CAN YOU OFFER TO THE WORLD?

In French-speaking Louisiana, the merchants have a time-honored custom of throwing in a little something extra with every purchase. "Lagnappe" the Louisianan's call it, and a merchant is judged largely by the amount of "Lagnappe" he gives with each purchase.

We of the big cities may smile at such childish customs, yet it is "Lagnappe" that accounts for most of the world's great successes.

When scales are divided evenly, just a very little extra will weigh down one side as much as would a thousand additional pounds. When merchandising or labor or service is standardized, just a very little extra value will make a man or an institution stand out head and shoulders above the crowd.

It is not by giving just what you are paid for that you win customers or make friends. It is the extra ounce of value or service that makes them remember you.

The mail order business is no different from any other in this respect. A little extra value, a premium or gift, will oftentimes double the response to your offer. Ask your reader for the privilege of sending your product to him for free examination, for instance, and you may get a satisfactory response, but offer him a worthwhile premium for doing you the favor of examining your product, and you'll get double the number of orders.

Here is the way it was done with Letterheads.

* * *

Will You Accept a "Black Beauty"
Fountain Pen and Pencil
With *My Compliments?*

Dear Sir:

With your permission, I am going to send to you a big, new "Black Beauty" Fountain Pen, and Pencil, oversize, self-filling, with 14-karat gold point, FREE!

And if you care to pay the small cost of engraving (only 15 cents), I'll have your full name die-stamped on it in solid gold leaf!

The circular enclosed shows you this beautiful new Fountain Pen and Pencil in its exact size. It looks as good and works as well as the pens which sell in stores at $3.00 to $5.00, and the makers guarantee it to give as satisfactory service. More than that, your name on it in letters of gold gives it a distinctiveness often lacking in high priced pens.

I am going to send this "Black Beauty" Fountain Pen and Pencil to you, just to get you to TRY our new Deluxe Letterheads and Envelopes, with your own name and address on them.

These new Deluxe Letterheads and Envelopes are coming to be regarded as the accepted form for social correspondence. To more quickly bring them into general use, we are going to give to a few representative people in each section, with their first order for 100 Letterheads and Envelopes, a genuine "Black Beauty" Fountain Pen and Pencil.

The regular price of the 100 Letterheads and Envelopes, with your name and address on them, is $2.00. If you mail the enclosed reservation at once, you get them for that same price, AND IN ADDITION, you get the "Black Beauty" Fountain Pen and Pencil FREE OF CHARGE!

This offer is good only on your first order. It is made merely to introduce the new Deluxe Letterheads and Envelopes. It will not be repeated. If you cannot mail the enclosed reservation at once, you might as well throw it away, for it is good for only ten days.

While those ten days last, however, you can get what is, we believe, as satisfactory a Fountain Pen and Pencil as there is on the market today, without one cent of cost, and with it 100 sheets and envelopes of distinctive, individual stationery.

Will you TRY them? Will you mail the enclosed Reservation on our guarantee that if you are not more than pleased; you have only to return them to get back your $2.00 in fully?

The day of bargains is almost over. This is your one and only chance to take advantage of one of the most unusual bargains yet offered.

Sincerely,

* * *

Anyone with a printing press can make up letterheads. Numbers of small-town printers have built up country-wide business on them by offering lower prices or more attractive letterheads than could readily be found elsewhere.

If your inclinations run towards printing, you can build a good clientele on letterheads. But unless you have something radically different in the way of design, your easiest method of landing new customers is to offer them an attractive premium, a Fountain Pen and Pencil as in the letter just quoted, or a Pencil or a key ring, or something likely to appeal to the class of reader you have in mind.

The big thing is to find a need, and then offer to fill it in a satisfactory way. It's amazing the things you can find to sell, when you look for the need. Amazing, too, how few words are needed at times.

Mark Foster sells pipes by mail, and does it highly successfully, yet his whole message could be hand-written on a postcard.

* * *

"I will gladly send you a Dr. Shotten Sanator pipe
for a 10 day absolutely free trial,
no money in advance, no C.O.D.

"If you don't say it's the greatest pipe you ever smoked
—regardless of the price—
BREAK IT UP, SEND ME THE PIECES,
AND OWE ME NOTHING."

* * *

A farmer selling "day-old" eggs prints his selling message on a Government postcard, and gets a goodly return in orders.

* * *

A Day-old Egg versus A "Strictly Fresh" Egg

Most eggs you buy as "Strictly Fresh," make four stops on their way to you. Each stop adds three or four days to their age. Yet these eggs are legally "Strictly Fresh" eggs.

COMPARE THESE WITH DATED EGGS, DELIVERED ONE DAY OLD

Eggs pure white, large and clean, shipped the very day they are laid, and safe arrival guaranteed! Time is the greatest factor in the flavor of an egg. An egg may be legally "fresh," but only an egg straight from the nest will give you that delightful taste which makes day-old table eggs so enjoyable. I collect my eggs every day, date them, then ship them the day they are laid, *and you get them just one day old!* Costs no more, because you save the profits of four middlemen. Zero cents a dozen *postpaid,* for pure white, large day-old Table Eggs. 3 dozen for $0.00.

Just Use the Order Form on the Other Side These Are Day-old Eggs, Try Them and Taste the Difference!

* * *

Perhaps the strongest offer of this type we have seen was that of a concern selling a "Hair-Restorer" Cream. Here is the way it read.

* * *

MEN, Here's a Contract
New Hair in 30 Days, Or No Cost!

Dear Reader:

This letter, coming to you in advance of any public announcement, is intended for your eyes alone. It contains information which we ask you to regard as confidential. You will see why in a moment.

For some time past, makers of certain high grade beauty creams have been flooded with complaints from women, claiming that their face creams stimulated the growth of the tiny hairs on the cheek and chin and upper lip.

These complaints became so general that a famous hair specialist was employed to examine into them. And here is what he found.

First, an examination of a number of women showed that the creams really had stimulated the hair growth to an amazing extent.

Second, analysis of all the creams complained of showed that in every case THESE CREAMS HAD AS THEIR BASE "LANOLIN," which is the fatty oil from the back of a sheep, or oil refined from sheep's wool.

Naturally, this started further investigations. Why should Lanolin stimulate hair growth? The reason was not far to seek. Since Lanolin is the oil you find in the fatty deposit right under the sheep's skin, it follows that Lanolin is the oil *which makes the sheep's own wool grow!*

The fact that human hair and sheep's wool both depend for their growth upon the fatty oil just under the skin has long been known to science. The reason for falling hair and baldness is equally well known . . ., *the drying up of these natural oils!*

This knowledge has led to hundreds of fruitless experiments with vegetable and mineral oils. They did not work, and the reason they did not is easy to understand.

You see, humans belong to the animal kingdom, and animal cells will absorb directly only animal oils. Vegetable or mineral oils will not nourish animal skin. So vegetable or mineral oils will not grow hair. BUT ANIMAL OILS WILL!

Under the direction of this famous Hair Specialist, samples of Lanolin Oil, refined by a special secret process, were distributed to hundreds of men and women, suffering from partial baldness. In almost every case where they were used, they put an immediate stop to excessive falling hair, and wherever there was a fine fuzz of hair on bald pates, this fuzz promptly grew and thickened and became healthy hair.

Men who had given up all hope of having hair again, grew thick, healthy heads of hair. It is believed that this discovery will eventually wipe baldness from the face of the earth!

For hair trouble is peculiar to the civilized races. Only 20% of it is caused by disease or infection. 80% is due to DRYING OF THE NATURAL OILS OF THE SCALP.

Tight hats are responsible for some of this; the lye or caustic soda in commercial soaps for a lot more, because these tend to dissolve and dry out the natural oils. The remedy?

1. Cleansing the scalp with a pure, animal oil soap, free from all lye and caustic soda.

2. Feeding the scalp and roots of the hair with specially refined Lanolin Oil.

We can't promise you, of course, that even the best Lanolin Oil will grow hair on a billiard ball, or on a scalp from which every trace of "fuzz" has disappeared. Where any of that fuzz remained, however, properly prepared Lanolin Oil has in practically every case in which it was tried, grown a healthy, thick crop of hair.

Whether it will grow hair for you, we do not know. All we can promise you is this; either it will grow new hair for you in 30 days, or it will cost you nothing.

One bottle of our extra strength especially prepared Lanolin Scalp Food . . ., a month's supply . . ., will either grow new hair for you, or convince you that it is hopeless. And one bottle costs only $1.98, plus the small postage charges. That $1.98 is not ours, however, until you say so. It goes right back to you, if you ask for it within 60 days.

Will you TRY a bottle of our extra strength Lanolin Oil, especially prepared Scalp Food, if I send it to you subject to 30 days' trial, your money to come back to you in full if the trial is not satisfactory? Will you mail the attached coupon on our hard and fast guarantee? A guarantee which you would have no trouble in getting Uncle Sam's Post Office to see that we live up to.

> If Lanolin Scalp Food does not grow a satisfactory head of new hair *for* you within 30 days, or if for any reason you want your money back, you have only to ask for it within 60 days, and we will return it in full.

On that guarantee, will you try a month's supply of Lanolin? On that distinct understanding, will you mail the attached Coupon?

Sincerely,

* * *

And here was the order form that went with it:

This Amazing New *Way* To Grow Hair
Now Yours Subject to 30 Days' Trial

Coupon No. 71

Name

Address

On your unconditional guarantee that it will grow a new head of hair for me in 30 days, or cost me nothing, you may send me a bottle of LANOLIN SCALP FOOD made of specially refined, extra strength Lanolin Oil, sufficient for a full month's supply.

I agree to deposit with the Postman, when he delivers the bottle, the sum of $1.98, plus the small postage charges, on this distinct guarantee.

If Lanolin Scalp Food does not grow a satisfactory head of new hair for me within 30 days, or if for any other reason I want my money back, I have only to ask you for it within 60 days, and you will return it to me in full.

Name

Address

City   State

* * *

That offer, we are told, pulled amazingly well, but had to be discontinued because the Lanolin preparation did not produce anywhere near as satisfactory results as expected. If you could find a satisfactory Hair Restorer, a letter along the lines of the one just given should do well.

The Prophet of old gave the secret of all business success in his advice to the woman whose sons were about to be sold into bondage. "What have you in the house?" he asked her. And when told, "Naught save a pot of oil," he bade her borrow vessels from the neighbors and pour out the oil. And as long as there were containers in which to put it, the oil continued to flow. What have YOU in the house? What service have you to offer, what gift can you give? Remember, even if it be only a better mousetrap, the world will wear a path to your door.

Find a need, and then set about satisfying that need. That is the basis upon which every successful business is built, and yours is no different. Necessity, you know, is the mother of invention. Admiral Crichton, in a London town house, was merely a butler. Thrown upon his own resources on a South Sea Isle, he became a genius.

Men are like that. In those countries that are veritable Gardens of Eden, where Nature has given of her gifts with a lavish hand, man grows so lazy that it is difficult to get him to bestir himself even to prepare the food so bountifully spread before him.

Mankind is naturally lazy, indolent. To do too much for anyone is to rob him of his initiative and frequently to ruin his life. That is the reason so few sons of rich men ever succeed. They lack incentive. They have no *need* to work. And lacking that, they miss the strongest urge in life.

It is only when we have to bestir ourselves or go without, that we wake up the spirit in us and use our talents to get the utmost out of whatever material is available to us.

Alaska and Switzerland are good examples of this. Alaska has enormous resources of gold and silver and copper and coal, vast virgin forests, 1,000,000 square miles suitable for agriculture, and the greatest fisheries in the world. Yet if Alaska were as densely populated as Switzerland, it would be supporting 120,000,000 people.

The Swiss have few natural resources, so they are constrained to use their ingenuity instead. They take a pound of steel wire, worth perhaps a dollar, and turn it into watch springs worth thousands. They take cotton thread at 20 cents a pound, and convert it into lace worth $200 a pound. They take a block of wood worth 10 cents and turn it into a carving worth $100. And because as a nation they have learned the art of using what they have to the best advantage, they have prospered amazingly.

The moral? That difficulties are given us to bring out the best that is in us. Like Jacob wrestling with the angel, we must not let them go until we have made them bless us—until, in other words, we have learned something worth while from them.

Difficulties, handicaps, obstacles, these are the steppingstones to success. They are the incentives that bring out the best that is in us.

> "One ship drives East, and another drives West,
> With the self-same winds that blow.
> 'Tis the set of the sails and not the gales
> Which tell us the way they go.
> Like the waves of the sea are the ways of Fate
> As we voyage along through life.
> 'Tis the set of the Soul which decides its goal
> Arid not the calm or the strife."
>
> Ella Wheeler Wilcox

Million Dollar Sales Letters
For Your Own Use and Profit

INTRODUCTION

Selling by mail can be the easiest and least expensive method of selling your services or commodities. It can also be the most difficult and the most expensive method of doing the job. It all depends on the method you use in presenting your offering to your prospects; it depends on the kind of a letter you send to them.

To write such a letter, a message that explains concisely yet completely and in an action-compelling manner what you have to offer, is a job that demands the services of an expert versed in every one of the thousand phases of selling and one with many years of successful mail order experience at his command.

If you would choose the one man in the United States who could write for you a sales letter that would produce the results you desire, you would probably ask Robert Collier to do the job. Backed by many years of success in the field of selling by mail, selling every commodity from trench machinery to fertilizers, books and raincoats, stocks and bonds and services, he has placed hundreds of millions of dollars into the pockets of the clients for whom he has written his master sales letter. As a consequence, he is today, America's premier writer of successful selling letters.

We asked Mr. Collier to select from the many thousands of sales letters considered the best of them all. It was a difficult job to pick fifteen of the best from a list of ten thousand of the best, but the job is finished and here are the letters. These are the fifteen letters considered the best ever written by the man acknowledged to be the best writer of sales letters in America today. They have been actually tested, they have been actually used, they actually sold over one million dollars of services and merchandise.

These letters will sell for you. Choose those which are applicable to your own business. Alter them only to such an extent as to accord with the products and services you have to sell. But it will pay you, too, to study them all, for they all contain the essential elements that enter into every successful sales letter. They contain ideas that you may apply successfully in sales letters of your own dictation.

LETTER # 1

THE LOWLY PENNY WILL OFTEN DO THE TRICK

Here is a letter to which a new penny was pasted. In conjunction with the figures given, the penny aroused an amazing amount of attention.

The idea could readily be used by Insurance Companies, Savings Banks and the like. It was also used with unusual results by an association trying to build a membership for the purpose of cutting the cost of government.

* * *

IT IS A MARVELOUS THING
The Power of Money to Make More Money!

Just this little insignificant penny, saved each week since the start of the Loan and Saving Association, would today amount to $75 - and of that $75, $50 WOULD BE INTEREST DIVIDENDS.

$1.00 saved each week would today amount to $7,500! THAT IS THE WAY MONEY GROWS!

No matter what his beliefs, every man will agree that the Scriptures contain some of the oldest and greatest truths known to mankind. There is one truth that the Wise Men of old felt to be so important, that they repeated it no less than six times in the very first chapter of the Bible, and referred to it throughout both Old and New Testaments.

This age-old truth is that EVERYTHING INCREASES AFTER ITS KIND! Plant a seed of corn, and you reap ears of corn. Plant thistles, and you grow a profusion of thistles. Plant money, and your money comes back to you after many days, increased a hundred-fold!

What harvest do YOU want to reap ten or fifteen years from now? Money to put your children through college, or start them in a business of their own? Security for yourself? Financial Independence?

You have only to set your goal in order to win it. The price of $5,000 or of $50,000 is only so many seeds of savings. $5.00 saved each week at the Loan and Savings Association will in about 13 Years amount to $5,000, $25 each week will grow to $25,000.

And mind you, here is the part that counts. Of that $25,000 only $16,250 represents money paid in by you. The rest - $8,750 - is GROWTH INCREASE!

Do you know any other way you can buy $25,000 as surely, as safely - and pay so little for it? Do you know any way you can buy $25,000 or any other sum, and pay for it in little, convenient installments each week that never depreciates in value, which are like seeds sown in good ground that keep growing and growing, year after year, always ready to give you more than you sow.

How much do you want to buy - $1,000 - $5,000 - $25,000? How much do you want to give to your youngster when he goes to college, or gets married, or starts in business? Here is the one sure and easy way of having that money when you want it. $1.00 a week now, means $1,000 thirteen years from now. $5.00 a week means $5,000.

What will you start with - $1.00 - $5.00 - $10.00? "To begin", says Ansonius, "it is to be half done".

Will you begin NOW - TODAY? Will you fill out the little form attached, pin your check, dollar bills or stamps to it covering your first remittance and mail it back in the enclosed envelope? Will you save the first $1.00 on your $1,000, or the first $25 on your $25,000 TODAY?

Sincerely,

* * *

LETTER # 2

HOW HANDKERCHIEFS WERE SOLD BY MAIL

A few years ago, a merchant in the clothing business in Buffalo failed. While he was waiting for the bankruptcy proceedings to be closed, he had no money and little credit. But he did have a family, and he had to do something to keep them from starving.

So he got a friend to advance him a few dollars and with that he bought some cheap knitted ties, and started mailing them, without orders of any kind to lists of likely buyers. With the ties, he sent a letter, offering the ties at 50 cents apiece, and enclosing postage for their return or for remittance.

Within a few months he is said to have cleared $200,000. In five years, it is reported that he made a couple of million. Similar offers were speedily made by dozens of other concerns. Here is the letter that successfully sold some hundreds of thousands of initialed handkerchiefs by this unique method.

* * *

Here's the most unusual offer
you've ever received.

For years, it's been the custom among well-dressed men who were fastidious about their handkerchiefs to have BOTH their initials embroidered on them. But up to now, they've always had to order them specially at considerable expense. For there were so many combinations of initials (630 to be exact) that no store could possibly carry them all in stock.

The result has been that fine quality handkerchiefs individually monogrammed have cost from 75 cents to $1.00 each. (Your wife will quickly verify this.)

Now, we've conceived the idea of monogramming handkerchiefs without orders (in quantities that would keep the cost low) and sending them by mail to a carefully selected list of Business Men who would appreciate the wonderful opportunity afforded them.

You are one of the men we selected. Your handkerchiefs are enclosed, four of them monogrammed especially for you WITH BOTH YOUR OWN INITIALS.

These handkerchiefs are of fine quality, are fully-sized, 18 inches square and have a neatly hemstitched border. You will readily see that such handkerchiefs should cost 75 cents each when specially embroidered in silk with your initials.

If you'd like to keep these handkerchiefs, send us not 75 cents each, not over 50 cents each - ONLY $1.00 FOR THE WHOLE FOUR. You can easily do it by slipping your check or money order in the enclosed envelope.

But, if you don't want to keep the handkerchiefs, just put them back in the envelope, paste the enclosed label and stamp over the address and shoot them back to us.

Isn't that a fair way to do business? It's the only way we know in which individually initialed handkerchiefs can be sold so reasonably.

When you send us the $1.00, in full payment for the handkerchiefs, please do not return the label with the stamp attached. Thank you! Every penny counts in selling handkerchiefs in this unusual way.

Yours for unusual handkerchief value,

P.S. There's a birthday or anniversary coming up soon for some man you know, and you'll be looking for just such an attractive gift as those individually monogrammed handkerchiefs. Why no double the amount of your remittance now, tell us his initials, and we'll get the handkerchiefs off at once - either to him or to you!

* * *

LETTER # 3

CAN HIGH PRICED ARTICLES BE SOLD BY MAIL?

YES, though it is necessary to first use the inquiry-bringing type of letter to winnow out the few interested people, and then keep after those few with a whole series of letters until you land their orders.

$25,000,000 worth of yachts were sold by mail this way. Inquiry-bringing letters and mailing pieces were mailed to them first, then to those interested, a series of letters and booklets were sent, and where possible personal calls were made.

Here is a letter which was most successful in bringing inquiries for a machine selling for about $2,500. It was mailed to a restricted field, Public Service Companies and it brought interested inquiries in considerable volume.

* * *

When Millions Were Actually

THROWN IN THE GUTTER!

"The most expensive gutters in the world" that is what they called the canals of 1830 which cost $200,000,000 to build and were doomed by the locomotive. What do you suppose they will call the trenches of today, where whole gangs of laborers, take days to dig up stretches of expensively paved streets, just to lay pipes and cables or drains under them?"

"The most expensive ditches in the world", probably. For these same holes could be bored at a tenth of the cost with a Hydrauger.

All the work of tearing up paving, all the expense of resurfacing, might just as well be thrown into the ditch, for all the need there is of it or all the good you get out of it.

You see, the HydrAuger bores UNDER the street. It can make any size hole from 2 ¼ inches to 10 ½ inches. It can bore any length up to 120 ft. It works as fast as a foot a minute, AND IT COSTS ONLY 10 CENTS TO 30 CENTS A FOOT!

"In 1930, we made plans for installing water mains in a newly incorporated borough", writes the Richland Township Water Co. of Windber, PA, "through which passes three paved highways. Our permit was conditioned upon NOT BREAKING THE PAVED SURFACE OF THE HIGHWAY. Thirty or more crossings were necessary. The HydrAuger enabled us to do the work in 1931 at minimum expenditure. We know of no better or more economical machine for its purpose. We completed the job for less than half the estimated cost of tunneling."

We can save more than half for you, too. May we tell you how? Your name on the enclosed card will bring full information by mail, without obligation.

Sincerely,

* * *

LETTER # 4

THEY SAID IT COULDN'T BE DONE

Have you ever tried to sell fertilizer, shrubbery and the like to suburbanites? It is not easy at the best of times, but during the depression, when you couldn't get rid of real estate for love or money, and when the mortgage companies were taking over homes right and left, selling fertilizer and such for the lawns was a real problem. Yet it was done. And here is one letter that did it with amazing success.

* * *

How To End Worries Over Scraggly Lawns

Dear Neighbor:

With your permission, I am going to make an analysis of the soil of your lawn to determine, at my own risk and expense, what elements are lacking in it, what you need for stronger, healthier, more closely grown turf.

Mind you, this will not cost you a penny or obligate you in any way. I am going to make this analysis just to show you how little is needed to correct the texture of your soil and make possible the growing of rich, thick grass.

You see, soil gets acid or alkaline such as your body does. Let your body become too acid and the results are quickly apparent in sallow skin, eruptions, disease. Let the soil of your lawn become too acid and the grass on it will quickly grow sallow, faded, full of weeds and noxious growths. But that condition can be quickly corrected - the missing elements easily added - once you have determined what the trouble is.

Will you let us make a chemical analysis of the soil in your lawn - and send you a report of it, WITHOUT COST OR OBLIGATION TO YOU?

John Smith of Jamestown, VA, wrote us:

"I should never have believed it possible that so slight a changing of the treatment of the soil could so quickly rebuild and re-establish a lawn. Your analysis showed us how to work wonders with our place."

Just your name on the enclosed card will bring you a FREE chemical analysis of your soil condition, with clear directions as to just what elements are needed to supply anything now lacking. A similar analysis from any chemist would cost several dollars.

Analysis will be made in the order in which requests are received, so if you would like to get your orders quickly, please mail your card NOW or telephone.

Sincerely,

* * *

LETTER # 5

A 100,000 MARK NOTE

To show how readily you can adapt to your business an idea that has been used successfully in some other line, here is an adaptation of the "Dollar Letter". (See Letter #10.)

Pinned to the top of this letter was a 100,000 mark German note. Its purpose, like that of the dollar, was to get the reader's immediate attention and arouse his interest in the message of letter.

It worked so well that the Wall Street Journal, for whom the letter was written, reported that it was the most successful subscription-getter they had ever used.

* * *

Will You Accept The Enclosed

German Reichsbank Note For 100,000 Marks,

With Our Compliments?

Dear Sir:

If the enclosed German Reichsbank Note for 100,000 Marks pays for one minute of your time, consider yourself engaged.

Yes, it's a real Reichsbank Note, put out by the German Government. Before the War, 100,000 marks were worth $23,820.00 in our money.

But when this particular issue of notes was retired, it took 10,000,000 notes like this to get a mark worth 24 cents in gold!

That is what uncontrolled inflation did to German money. As fast as new issues were brought out, the old ones dropped in value, until a man's only chance to get ahead lay in putting his money in common stocks, or into goods or real estate - or something that would go up in price just as fast as the value of his money went down.

In a small way, something of the kind may occur here. Even with inflation under perfect control, the value of the inflated money is bound to drop, while common stocks and goods and real estate will go up in value.

The question is - what type of stocks will depreciate most? And what effect will inflation have upon various lines of industry?

That is where the Blank Street Journal can be of genuine help to you. Its facts are not merely timely, but they are derived from original sources, and their accuracy can be depended upon. But that isn't all. The facts it brings to you each day are interpreted from the standpoint of the investor and of the business man, enabling you to invest your money or to plan your business with understanding and foresight.

The Blank Street Journal is the source of information for countless statisticians, newspapers and market services. Yet the information for which you pay the high fees is just as readily available to you in the pages of the daily Blank Street Journal, as it is to them.

The enclosed card entitles you to the next SIXTY ISSUES of the Blank Street Journal for $3. Not only that, but it brings you FREE EXAMINATION of the first five copies. If these five do not make clear to you the financial trend, if they do not show you every phase of business and financial activity, just tell us to cancel, and you will be out nothing.

Will you TRY it? Will you let us send you accurate news from the very heart of the financial center of the country NOW - when that news may be worth more to you than ever in your lifetime? Will you mail the enclosed form TODAY?

Sincerely,

* * *

LETTER # 6

CLOSE OUTS

End of the Season Sales are the plague of every merchant. How to clean out the remnants of stock at a price that will appeal to the public and still leave a modicum of profit is something to make any advertising man rack his brain.

Here is a letter that we used first on books. When the Simond's War History sale was over, there were a couple of thousand returned or damaged sets on hand. The price was reduced to 25 cents and a letter along the lines of the attached was mailed. It pulled so well that the 2,000 sets were disposed of at once, and the order cost was found to be so low that it paid to deliver some 6,000 brand new sets on the orders that came in.

Adapted to Traveling Bags, the letter did just as well. Here it is, used to dispose of the odds and ends of a stock of Overcoats. It has been successful on every product on which we have used it.

* * *

790 Leftover Ulsters At A Big Discount!

Dear Sir:

In the rush and excitement of selling, in the past two months, of 21,000 "Keep Warm" Winter Ulsters, there was no time to pay attention to exactly how sizes and colors were running.

The result is that now, with the season near its end, we find ourselves with 790 coats left over (in all sizes) but without a complete range of sizes in any one color.

There are dark grays and blues and beautiful brown heather-mixtures, in Greatcoats that we sold in the past all the way up to $47.00 - really handsome colors, all of them - but we can't be sure of having your exact size in the color you specify.

And you know how the Overcoat season is - if these Ulsters are not all disposed of before Christmas, some of them will probably be on our hands until next Fall.

So rather than carry any of them over until then, we have decided to make one sweeping reduction, and offer these 790 smart, distinctive, beautifully tailored Greatcoats of fine, warm, double-texture pure wool cloth - for only $27.65!

This is the lowest price we have ever made on these all-wool "Keep Warm" Ulster Coats. Just try to find their equal in style, in workmanship, in fine quality material for $40 or $50.

* * *

Only 790 Coats Left

We have just 790 of these double-texture all-wool Greatcoats to sell at this low price. When they are gone, your chance to save on your Winter Ulster will go with them. But while these 790 last, you can get as perfect-fitting, as good-looking, as fine-quality a Winter Greatcoat as ever you would want to wear, at an almost unheard-of bargain.

If you will just write your name and three simple
measures on the enclosed card and mail to us, we will
send you a "Keep Warm" Ulster, that will exactly fit
you, by prepaid Parcel Post.

You may keep the overcoat for a full week. Then, if
for ANY REASON AT ALL you don't care to keep
the coat, you can send it back AT OUR EXPENSE.
But if you are so well-pleased with it that you don't
want to part with it, just send us $27.65, the low price
at which we are offering these last remaining 790
coats.

SEND NO MONEY - simply mail the post card. But
do it at once, this opportunity to save money will not
occur again.

Yours up to 790,

PRESIDENT

* * *

LETTER # 7

USING A PREMIUM

When you want to land a fish, you bait your hook with something that the fish likes. When you want to land a lot of orders, the same principle applies.

A client wanted to sell a new, small size traveling bag. He tried selling it on its merits alone, and got 3% to 4% of orders. Since the bag sold for $7.95, and 3% gave him an order cost of only $1.00, that was profitable. But he wanted volume.

So he tried using a bit of bait. To all who would send for this new bag, he offered a Fountain Pen with their name die-stamped on it in letters of gold. Instead of only 3% or 4%, that attractive bait brought the orders up to 10%, 12% and even on some lists, to 14%.

$$* * *$$

Will you accept one of the latest model, self-filling Fountain Pens with your name die-stamped in raised letters upon it, in return for a little favor I want you to do?

The courtesy is a small one, pleasant and easy to render.

For years, you know, the standard size Traveling Bag has been an 18 inch bag like the famous "Twentieth Century Bag", but lately many friends have been writing that they would like a bit smaller bag than this - something light and inexpensive, but with all the strength and fine appearance, all the unique conveniences of the "Twentieth Century".

Now we are trying one out - a bag so convenient that we don't believe its equal has ever been made before - certainly not anywhere near the price.

Every time you pack this Bag, you will be thankful for the TIME-SAVING convenience of its wonderful interior pockets. It has a place for everything you need on a trip - and it almost "packs itself".

Ever have toothpaste or shaving cream get all over your clean shirts and collars? Or the stopper come out of a bottle and the contents run over everything?

Then you'll appreciate the convenience of the moisture-proof pockets lined with the long-wearing, high grade hospital rubber. No moisture can leak through it.

These five moisture-proof pockets will hold shaving gel, talcum powder or toilet water - all your toilet needs.

On the opposite side of the bag are two full-length pockets with folders for carrying shirts, ties, underwear, socks, and any papers that you need when you go on a trip.

These handy pockets are collapsible and take up no room when not filled. They not only enable you to pack your bag in half the time it used to take, but they keep all your things shipshape, and leave the entire bottom part of the bag free to pack suits of clothes and other large articles. A wealth of packing space.

I am writing a few of our customers for their opinion of these new Traveling Bags. We call them "RedypaktBags" because they're handy for so many different uses.

I would like you to try one of them for a week - USE it on your next trip - see how convenient, how time saving, how handsome it is. Compare it with bags you have paid $12 or $15 for. And then tell me what you and your friends think of it.

It is a small favor, but it means a great deal to me. We are thinking of making a general offering of these "RedypaktBags" all over the country, but before doing it, I would like to have your opinion.

Just your name on the enclosed card will bring a "RedypaktBag" to you to try out for a week FREE. At the end of the week, if you should like the BAG so well that you want to keep it for your own, you can have it for only $7.95. If you don't want to keep it, please send it back at my expense, telling me what you think about it, and I'll be deeply grateful to you.

Naturally, this special price holds good only if your card comes in at once, while your advice will still be of value to us.

Won't you, therefore, put your name on the card and mail it now? I thank you for your courtesy.

Gratefully yours,

P.S. The new model, sell-filling fountain pen which I'll send along will have your name die-stamped upon it. And whether or not you keep the "RedypaktBag", I want you to keep the pen as a present from me, entirely free of charge. It's a return for your courtesy in examining the "RedypaktBag" and giving me your opinion about it.

* * *

LETTER # 8

AN INDIRECT APPROACH

The longest way around is frequently the shortest way home, when it comes to selling people an idea.

If we were to come to you, and tell you that we'd be glad to put your name in some "Who's Who" provided you would dig up $10 for a copy, you'd shy off at once. It would be too apparent that the only reason we were listing you was to get your $10.

But if we approach you tactfully and indirectly, there is a good chance we shall get both your listing and your $10. Here is an example of the indirect approach that worked well.

* * *

Dear Madam:

Would you be good enough to do me a favor? I promise not to ask too much.

You can help to solve a problem which is of significance to all officials of Women's clubs. You know that for 34 years, the leading Club Women of the United States have been recorded each year in the So & So of Women's Clubs.

This year, a symposium is being conducted among the leading officials of Women's Clubs, to determine whether it would add measurably to the So & So's value to include an entirely new section, a "Who's Who Among Club Women", giving a short biographical sketch with the offices you have held and all the outstanding achievements of your Club life.

Your Club Activities entitles you to representation in this exclusive section. Will you be good enough to give me your opinion of the value of a section?

There will be no charge for the listing, but since each listing will mean considerable additional expense in the way of typesetting and the like, we shall ask each of those whose biographical sketches appear in this "Who's Who" to subscribe for one copy of So & So. To make up for this however, we shall send it to them - not at the regular price of $5.00, but at a special pre-publication discount of 15% - making the net price to them $4.25, and even from this figure we shall give them an additional discount for advance payment.

We shall greatly appreciate an expression of your opinion from you. If that opinion is favorable, please fill out the Record attached, giving your Club connection and all those little personal items that Society Editors and others ask for, when you own or your club's activities bring your name into the news.

The enclosed envelope needs no stamp. Won't you, therefore fill out the Record NOW - while it is in your hands and mail it right back in the enclosed envelope?

Thank you!

Appreciatively,

* * *

LETTER # 9

BARGAINS

Everyone offers bargains, at least, everyone claims that if you take into consideration the quality and so on of his product, it is a bargain at this price.

But what everyone claims, no one believes. So you've got to do more than claim that your price is low or you offer an unusual bargain. You've got to show the reason why.

Here is a letter that was unusually successful in convincing readers that they were getting something unusual in the way of price reduction, and therefore brought back their orders in profitable quantities.

* * *

Mr. Business Man:

"Name your own price!" said the manufacturer.

And we did.

You know how most factories are - busy and working overtime eight or ten months of the year and idle the rest. And those idle months, like the famines of ancient Egypt, eat up most of the profits of the busy ones.

We offered to keep this factory busy making new Carozy Robes all during the idle season.

"Name your own price", was the answer.

We named a price. It was accepted without cavil or question, with the result that we can offer you, at $9.85, a Motor Rob that customers tell us could not be equaled in stores at anywhere near that price. The folder enclosed will give you some idea of the beauty and richness of this luxurious Robe.

Naturally, bargains like this won't last long. We got this one manufacturer's output for three months, but while three months' output is a lot of robes, they won't go far among our more than 300,000 customers.

The enclosed card will bring one of these beautiful new Carozy Robes to you for a week's examination, FREE! No money, no risk, no obligation. Just the postcard.

"A direct saving to me of at least $7.50," wrote John Smith of Clarksburg, WV, when he saw his robe.

The card will be worth good money to you, too, IF YOU WILL MAIL IT AT ONCE.

Yours for mutual cooperation,

PRESIDENT

* * *

LETTER # 10

THE DOLLAR LETTER

Here is the most successful letter we have ever heard of, the famous "Dollar Letter". Pinned to its top was a crisp, new dollar bill, a real dollar bill.

This letter pulled better than a 90% response. The writer of this letter told us that from 175,000 mailed, he got back $270,000, plus more than 90% of the $1.00 bills mailed out with them.

But this was only the start. From the list of more than 150,000 people who gave that $270,000, further subscriptions were secured to the amount of nearly $14,000,000.

* * *

Dear Mr. Jones:

Here's a dollar: Yes, it's a REAL dollar, nice and clean and new.

Keep it if you want to, after you've read this letter, but I don't believe you will, then.

Here's what it's all about:

I've made an investment of a thousand dollars in human nature and human kindness. I've mailed a thousand dollars, in a thousand letters, to a thousand people picked at random. I have done this because I believe that every one is really kind, way down inside - that no one is REALLY heartless and that the only reason why folks do not help where help is needed is just because these needs are not IMPRESSED upon them hard enough.

"And that's the mission of each of my thousand dollars, to impress the importance of a need. This thousand dollars is my subscription to the Blank Hospital, and I'm investing in the belief that every one will bring back several more (at least another) with it. So our subscription, which I'm starting in this way will be at least two thousand, maybe five, for there's going to be a lot of you who will send a five or a ten or more, when you mail my dollar back.

Remember, both my dollar and your dollars go to help crippled children.

Will EVERY ONE come back?

Will everyone bring something more?

Are people really kind - or REALLY heartless?

Have I made a good investment?

What is YOUR answer?

Sincerely,

* * *

LETTER # 11

SELLING SECURITIES BY MAIL

How about selling stocks by mail? Millions of dollars of such sales have been made, and when properly done, it is one of the least expensive methods of selling known.

The easiest way, of course, is to send an inexpensive letter to your list first, to find out who can be interested in that particular type of investment. To those who answer that letter, you can afford to send a whole series of follow-ups, booklets or make a personal call.

Here is a type of letter which has met with marvelous success in offers of this kind.

* * *

Here Is The Industry That Started

MANY OF THE GREAT FORTUNES OF TODAY!

Dear Sir:

Men made iron and steel for thousands of years. Along came a new process and a man named Carnegie to capitalize it, and made a thousand millionaires. When "in steel" while this magic change was in process, made fortunes almost overnight.

Men have been brewing beer for thousands of years. Along came Prohibition and practically closed the industry. Breweries were dismantled, their working crews scattered to the four winds.

BUT NOW, WITH A STROKE OF THE PEN PRESIDENT ROOSEVELT HAS CHANGED ALL THIS.   NOW, ALMOST OVERNIGHT, COMES A DEMAND FOR BEER GREATER THAN THE COUNTRY HAS EVER BEFORE KNOWN!

The stocks of the few active, well-equipped breweries soared overnight. In two weeks, they increased 48% in value, while the average of all stocks went up only 6%. Yet if the record of earnings means anything, that is only the start. Men with good brewery stocks should see them rise to almost phenomenal heights as did those "in steel" back in Carnegie's day. Breweries today should make even more.

Yet there is one brewery which has been in continuous operation in the same family for 77 years, with a splendid plant and a fine old name, and which has so far escaped the notice of stock market investors. To us, it seems to offer greater possibilities of profit from small investment than anything you can put your money into today.

May we tell you more about it?

Sincerely,

* * *

LETTER # 12

SECURING INQUIRIES FOR A BOOKLET

How can you most easily find the people interested in new courses, new sets of books and the like?

By offering to the most likely lists of prospects, to send without cost a booklet of interest only to people desiring that particular type of knowledge. The encyclopedia Britannica, for instance offers a booklet containing sample pages and illustrations from its new Encyclopedia. Collier's offers a booklet telling in the words of Dr. Eliot of Harvard what he considers the essentials of a liberal education, and thus finds the people who can be interested in Dr. Eliot's Five Foot Shelf of Books.

Here is such a letter, designed to winnow out from the other lists the names of all those interested in learning the art of Public Speaking. It is one of the most successful inquiry-bringing letters we have used.

* * *

Now For The First Time —

"THE SECRET OF EFFECTIVE SPEECH" - FREE!

Dear Sir:

At your request, I shall be glad to send you one of the most talked-of little books ever written. It will cost you exactly one cent - the price of the stamp that will bring the enclosed card back to me.

The name of this booklet is, *"The Secret of Effective Speech"*. The principal part of it was written by perhaps the most successful speaker of modern times, the man who made over $4,000,000.00 from his lectures, and then used it to send young men through College - Russell Conwell, author of "Acres of Diamonds".

"The Secret of Effective Speech" should be read by every executive who ever has to face a hostile audience, whether that audience consists of one man or a thousand.

It is not made up of rules and principles, but of the few common-sense essentials which Conwell found of most importance in his thousands of appearances on the public platform. It is radical. It is stimulating. AND IT IS FREE!

Your name and address on the enclosed card will bring you a copy of *"The Secret of Effective Speech"*, with out compliments. You will like this little book. It is short, but there is a tremendous lot in it. Every time you read it, you will realize more clearing why Russell Conwell had so many thousand enthusiastic admirers, who audiences hung upon his every word.

Frankly, we are taking this means of bringing to the attention of a few alert business executives a new method of teaching Public Speaking - a method so striking and simple, yet so amazingly successful, that it is taking the country by storm.

Will you use the postcard NOW - TODAY?

Sincerely,

* * *

LETTER # 13

SPORTS APPEAL - SALES APPEAL

Sports articles are notably successful in mail selling, where you can get lists of people interested in any particular sport. Fishing tackle, golf clubs and balls, tennis racquets and a host of other products have been successfully sold by mail. There is even a concern in Baltimore which sells fine saddlery by mail and has built a surprisingly profitable business.

Here is a letter that sold Field Glasses by mail, and sold them in goodly quantities. Its basic idea is just as applicable to dozens of other products that appeal to all sportsmen.

* * *

Now the Far Distances are Yours
WITH MAGIC EYES THAT SEE FOR MILES!

Dear Friend:

Here is a wonderful way to add to the enjoyment of your trips, to give you "ring side" seats at every sporting event, to bring anything you want to see within a few feet of you MULTIPLYING YOUR OWN EYE-SIGHT BY THE POWER OF THESE EIGHT MAGIC LENSES!

Four-Mile Eyes - that is what they give you, spanning distances like the fabled seven-league boots of childhood. For the hunter, they are a necessity. For the tourist or traveler, they add a zest that doubles the enjoyment of sightseeing. For those who love sports, they make a nearby window or hilltop as desirable as the most expensive "ring side" seat.

Yet for a little while, they can be had FOR LESS THAN THE COST OF A SINGLE SEAT!

You see, the finest glasses in the world are made in Central Europe. And you know how conditions have been over there - many highly skilled artisans getting lenses for a month's toil than they would for a single day's work here. The result? Bargains as you will never get again. Bargains such as we never dreamed of being able to offer in Fine Field Glasses. Prices are higher over there now and are stiffening rapidly, but up to a few weeks ago, you could get the finest achromatic day and night lenses at figures so ridiculously low as to seem like a gift.

We had a lot of extra powerful Officer's Field Glasses shipped to us at those prices a month ago. They have just been unpacked and gone over, and they are beauties. Filled with specially large achromatic day and night lens, and equipped with compass and focusing scale. They are the most powerful glasses of the kind we have ever seen at anywhere near the price.

I have a pair on my desk before me as I write, and through them I can mount the high tension wires on a hill a couple of miles east of here, and through these glasses, I can watch every move of the builders. If they were football players, I could see them better than from the choicest seat.

And the reason? These glasses were made for the use of Army Officers, and they had to be good. They are the only 8-lens Galilean Field Glass with compass and leather case that sell for less than $30.00! But while they last, I am going to let you have a pair for $7.95!

Not only that, but if you mail the enclosed card right away, I will send them to you, postpaid, for a week's FREE EXAMINATION and TRIAL!

SEND NO MONEY! Just your name and address on the enclosed card will bring a pair of these extra-powerful, *-lens Officer's Field Glasses to you at our risk, our expense, TRY them! Test them against the finest glasses you can find selling at $30.00 to $40.00 a pair. If these are not clear, stronger, more satisfactory in every way, send them back. If you are willing to part with them for any reason, send them back. Otherwise, $7.95 makes them your own, an endless source of pleasure and usefulness. On that understanding, will you TRY a pair of these Magic Eyes? With that distinct agreement, will you put your name on the enclosed card, and mail it NOW? You will never have another such opportunity.

Sincerely,

* * *

LETTER # 14

USING PRESSURE

Want to start a business of your own by mail? Here is a letter that brought in more than $1,000,000.00 worth of orders for a new concern in its first six months.

Every man wants to make money. Every man wants to see his money grow. When you start by asking your reader if he'd like to see one dollar grow to a hundred, you have his attention. when you prove to him that he can learn how to work such a miracle before he pays out a single penny, you are sure of his interest. After that, the bringing back of the actual order is mere detail.

This letter is high-pressure... to much so for many projects - but for those that can stand it, it embodies every feature of the successful selling letter.

* * *

My dear Sir:

Would you like to see $1.00 grow to $60.00, $8.00 grow to $500.00 by next March?

Let me tell you how:

I am going to send you within the next few days a set of seven little books. These books are probably not like any you have ever seen before because:

They are about YOU!

They show you that you have been using but a small part of your real abilities - that back in your subliminal mind", as the scientists call it, is a sleeping Giant who. awakened, can carry you on to fame and fortune almost overnight! A Genie-of-your-Brain as powerful, as capable of satisfying your every wish, as was ever Aladdin's wonderful Genie-of-the-lamp of old.

They make your Day Dreams, your visions of wonderful achievement, of fortune, health and happiness COME TRUE - not five, ten, or fifteen years from now, but TODAY, A.D. 1925!

I am going to send these little books to you - with no obligations on your part, for you to read and ACTUALLY TRY OUT for a week at my risk and expense.

But - there's just one thing - I don't want to send these without first getting your permission. You can grant that in a moment on the enclosed special "Courtesy Card".

When I send the books, there's absolutely no obligation on your part to pay for them. You can return them for ANY reason, or for no reason at all.

BUT HERE'S THE MOST IMPORTANT PART!

If you; find these little books are everything I say about them (and you're to be the sole judge), how much would you expect to pay for them? $30.00? $50.00? $100.00? That's what ordinary courses, which merely promise to show you how to do some special kind of work, cost you. Certainly, if this one will do the half of what I've promised you, it will be worth all of that - and more!

Well - if you decide to keep these books, you need send me - NOT $50.00 or $100.00, not even their regular price of $13.50 - but my SPECIAL INTRODUCTORY PRICE TO YOU, good only on this ADVANCE EDITION of $6.85! (If you prefer the more convenient monthly payments, send only $1.00 a month for eight months.)

And that isn't all!

If within 6 months your $1.00 hasn't grown to $60.00, if you can't credit to the $6.85 you pay for this Course at least $500.00 of ADDITIONAL EARNINGS, send back the books and I'll refund to you cheerfully and in full every cent you have paid to me for them.

There are no conditions - no strings attached of any kind to this offer. If within 6 months these little books have not brought you the pot of gold at the foot of the rainbow, then they are not for you. Send them back and get your money!

* * *

LETTER # 15

USING THE "YOU" ELEMENT

There is a concern in one of the Eastern states which built a business running into the millions on four letters. Those four letters were used over and over again, year after year. They finally wore out, but after several years' rest, they are again good for an occasional mailing.

All those letters were built around the most important and interesting subject you can write about to any reader - HIMSELF.

Here is the most successful of these four letters - "Will you give me a little information about YOURSELF?"

* * *

Dear Sir:

Will you give me a little information about yourself, just your height and weight?

I want to send you one of our famous "Rainproof" Coats (designed especially for substantial Business Men) for you to examine, free of charge; but I can't send one in your size without knowing your height and weight.

Over 36,000 Men-of-Affairs, in all parts of the country, wear these "Rainproof" Coats on rainy days. They are just the kind of coat EVERY well-dressed business man needs in the Spring and Fall, for they are really TWO COATS IN ONE - a perfect raincoat for stormy days and a well-appearing Topcoat for cold and windy days.

More than 36,000 keen business and professional men who have ordered "Rainproof" Coats during the past two years paid us prices varying from $17.85 to $23.50 for their coats.

NOW FOR ONE MONTH ONLY - WE ARE OFFERING THESE "RAINPROOF" COATS AT THE LOWEST PRICE AT WHICH THEY HAVE BEEN OFFERED IN THE TWO YEARS - $16.65!

From Ohio, Mr. John Jones, Vice-President and Treasurer of Blank Cement Co., writes:

"I never got as much comfort and satisfaction out of any coat as I have from the "Rainproof". I had been looking for such a garment for years - a coat I could wear on all occasions and be proud of."

And this is just one out of hundreds of letters and telegrams that have come from men who have ordered these "Rainproof" Coats and been delightedly surprised with their fine style, great usefulness and good value.

Won't you fill in your height and weight on the enclosed postcard, and mail it to me? Then I can send you one of these famous "Rainproof" Coats - in your exact size by Parcel Post for a week's FREE TRIAL. You can examine the coat at your leisure, with no insisting clerks at your side, and WEAR IT A FULL WEEK FREE. If you don't think it is just the kind of coat you've always wanted, just fire it back at MY EXPENSE, and accept my thanks for the privilege of sending it to you.

But remember - this is the only month in which we are going to offer "Rainproof" Coats at the special "lowest-in-years' price of $14.65!

Hadn't you better drop the postcard into the mail RIGHT NOW - while you can take advantage of this Special Offer?

* * *

Afterword

You hold in your hands a roadmap and blueprint to what could lay the foundation for your financial security. You may be familiar with the saying, "When the student is ready, the teacher will appear," and Robert Collier is one of the finest teachers of marketing and copywriting you could ever find.

You may be saying to yourself, "The world was simpler then, now we have the Internet, Blogs and Social Media." Well, Collier's tools were simple, a pen, a pencil, perhaps a typewriter and some paper, and he made a fortune for himself and his clients with them.

The principles you have learned, selling to human beings in a personal manner, are timeless and used today by thousands of Internet and direct marketers worldwide. The tools may change, but human nature has not.

Collier's methods and letters are not full of "hype." They are personal in nature, like you and a friend sitting down for a chat.

Although my personal journey began before I found, *"How To Make Make Money At Home In Spare Time By Mail,"* I like to believe that it is not coincidental that you are reading it now, and that I was the one to find this book for you when all others had forgotten it.

If you enjoyed the book or are a fan of Robert Collier, I would love to hear from you and learn your story. Contact me by visiting:

www.best-success-and-marketing-books.com

Bernie Malonson
Publisher

PS: It's a work in progress, so I hope you won't mind the dust.

Made in the USA